*To
the
World
of
Men,
Welcome*

Nuala Ní Chonchúir

*To
the
World
of
Men,
Welcome*

ARLEN
HOUSE

To the World of Men, Welcome

is published in 2011 by
ARLEN HOUSE
42 Grange Abbey Road
Baldoyle
Dublin 13
Ireland
Phone: +353 86 8207617
Email: arlenhouse@gmail.com

ISBN 978-1-85132-025-7, paperback

International distribution by
SYRACUSE UNIVERSITY PRESS
621 Skytop Road, Suite 110
Syracuse, New York
USA 13244-5290
Phone: 315-443-5534/Fax: 315-443-5545
Email: supress@syr.edu
www.syracuseuniversitypress.syr.edu

Typesetting by Arlen House
Cover Artwork 'Lovers and Feathers'
by Pauline Bewick

CONTENTS

ACKNOWLEDGEMENTS

The story 'Stitching Time' was shortlisted for both the Molly Keane and the Bill Naughton Awards in 2004 and published in the *Splinters* anthology. 'One Hare's Foot' was first published in *Southword* magazine. 'Jacques D'Arc's Dream' appeared in *Crannóg*. 'Ice' featured in *Ropes 2005*. 'Well Met, Well Met' was published in *Image* magazine. 'Toys' featured on *west47* online. 'I, Caroline' was first published in the anthology *¡DIVAS! A Sense of Place* and also in *Spiked* magazine (UK). 'Runt' featured in *The Irish Feminist Review*. 'Loveday' was shortlisted for the Bibliofemme Short Story Competition, and published on their website. 'Asylum' won the Dromineer Literary Prize and was published by Pen Pusher (UK). A version of 'From Life' was shortlisted for the Willesden Herald International Short Story Competition. 'The Ouse's Call' was published in *The Yellow Room* (UK).

A sincere and special thank you goes to Pauline Bewick for the beautiful art on the cover. I would like to thank Alan Hayes for his friendship and courage, Jonathan Williams for his perseverance, Marilyn Gaughan and all at the Arts Office in Galway County Council for their continued support, the Arts Council for the bursary which helped me to buy time to write, Órfhlaith Foyle for encouragement and goblin moments, Karen O'Neill for photos and fun, and my sons, Cúán and Finn, for their patience.

Míle buíochas ó chroí

Do mo dheartháireacha
Ronan & Declan,
mo dheirfiúracha
Maeve, Aoife & Úna,
agus do
John Dillon,
le buíochas

*To
the
World
of
Men,
Welcome*

THE LAST MAN

The last man she tumbled with was special: the whole of his back was made up of a tattoo of Our Lady of Guadalupe. He was a big fella – broad-backed – and the Virgin reclined across his skin, magnificent in her robin's-egg-coloured cloak and rosy gown. His shoulder-blades jutted through Our Lady's slender shoulders, and she was held up from the small of his back by the arms of a *putto*. Francine sighed when she saw the tattoo – she loved pictures of saints, they made her feel safe – and the Blessed Virgin, in each of her worldly guises, was one of her all-time favourites. She especially liked her in this, her Mexican form.

'Our Lady of Guadalupe', she whispered, fingering the image lightly, following the fall of the praying hands under tiny sprouts of back hair. Mick turned over in the bed and shoved the pillow under his head, so that he was propped over her.

'That's right', he said, looking into Francine's face, surprised that she had recognised the specific Virgin pictured in his tattoo.

'I love Holy Mary', she said, 'her face is kind'.

'Not unlike your own face', he said and smiled. 'Here, I've got more. Thérèse of Lisieux is down this leg'. And he kicked the quilt off to show her.

'Oh, isn't she just lovely, with her handful of roses? The Little Flower'. Francine touched the saint's brown habit, could feel its woolly texture as part of Mick's skin.

'Isn't she great?'

'She is'. Francine trailed her hand down his back. 'Have you been to Mexico, is that where you got the Guadalupe tattoo?' She was hoping for a vicarious thrill: the whiff of *mole*, drunken nights in Oaxaca, heat and dust and pale yellow light.

'No, the furthest from here I've ever been is England. I get them done in a tattoo place off Capel Street. Your man is very good'.

He giggled and kissed her with his juicy lips. While she licked her way up Our Lady of Knock's rosary beads – and Mick's right arm – Francine wondered if their shared love of Catholic icons might make them soul-mates. Maybe they'd go around markets and charity shops together, searching out plaster statues, buying bleeding Sacred Hearts and pictures of saintly now-you-see-them, now-you-don't apparitions. Then Mick whispered to her that he had to go. He laughed and said his wife would be wondering where the hell he was. Francine sighed again.

When he was gone, she ruffled her toes across the sheet, kicking away the crumbs, and listened to the alarm clocks on each side of the bed beating out their metronomic rhythm in stereo. One clock was hers, the other was long-gone-Roger's. She didn't know why she kept his. The two clocks ticked her life on and on in a way that drove her mad. She thought about Mick and what a pity it was that he was married. He had freckles dashed across his nose like rust spots on a gate; they looked lovely.

Marriage had made Francine invisible. On her wedding day – the loneliest day of her life – she had stared around the function room, at the grinning, gorging guests, and wondered what she'd done. She looked at her new husband and saw a bland imitation of the man she had first met. The

Roger she used to know was slim, lively and almost spontaneous. This one was a slug-like, selfish twit. Roger raised his wine-glass to her and the smile that she sent back to him pulled the skin across her face and hurt her cheeks.

Once they were married, Roger said that he didn't want her to work. It would be better for her to stay at home to look after the house and garden – less pressure. Francine had to admit that she'd done it willingly for a while. It was nice not to have to get up for work every morning, not to have to bother with make-up and getting clothes ready and endless office chit-chat. All that rot. She was never any good at small-talk – her tongue always became thick and stupid – she never seemed to be able to properly tune in to other people's conversations. Instead she was always on the edges, hovering like the static interference on a transistor radio. So, she became a housewife and piddled about at home, filling her days with the never-ending needs of their home.

And she waited. Francine waited and waited. But nothing happened: the babies she was waiting for didn't come. She got fed up faffing around with ironing and washing, endless cooking and tidying and hanging around. Doing and re-doing. Still Roger wanted her to stay at home.

'But there's nothing to do', she had protested.

'Nothing to do?' He laughed at her.

'I could go to college, learn a language or something. Spanish maybe'.

'Francine, I don't think you have the self-discipline for study, do you?'

'I'm bored, Roger, bored out of my head'.

'There's no such thing as bored', Roger said.

If Roger was finished talking, that was it, there was no point in arguing, so Francine swallowed herself up and disappeared. Her life wasn't much, she had nothing to do or to say, but she read a lot, lolled in bed a lot, thought a lot.

She thought about the way she used to have a sort of aerial view of her life. She could look down and see the how and the why of things, she could plot what would eventually happen, move herself into the right spot, like a puppet on a stage. Francine used to know the reason she did things – she used to *do* things – but she had lost her way.

She began to think about Roger. She thought about the fact that they never went anywhere together anymore, he never brought her out. Francine thought about his late nights (overtime), his dinners out (business meetings), his Sunday golf (networking), his trips abroad (business meetings 'away'), his address book full of women's names and numbers (clients). She thought it was time to call a halt. So she did.

Francine flumped down into the sofa with a notebook and made two lists. One list was headed 'Roger', the other 'Fantasy Man':

Roger	Fantasy Man
Good provider	Slapdash with money
Boring	Thinks I'm sexy
Nice looking	Is sexy himself
Likes golf	Likes booze and fags and motorbikes (maybe even drugs!)

Reading the lists aloud a few times, Francine wondered how honest either of them really was. She made a plan. I'm going to start enjoying myself, she thought. If Roger isn't around to take me out, I'll go by myself. For starters, Francine decided she would go to nightclubs – more anonymous than pubs – any night that Roger wasn't around. She'd go to nightclubs and look out for the Fantasy Man. Just to pass the time, just to give her something to think about while she Hoovered the floors and emptied the bins and filled the dishwasher. It would give her a bit of jizz, a little thing of her own to make her feel excited.

She went once a week to begin with – to *Rouge*, the nightclub in the next town – and soon, as often as she could manage it. At first she only danced, tossing herself into the music, eyes closed, lurching on the spot on the dance-floor, not even looking at the other bodies moving around her. She would throw her arms over her head and sway, losing all of herself in the music. Francine loved the sticky, beer-messed floor; the lights strobing like alien spaceships, the smoky night-time feel of it all. She enjoyed being part of another world, one that had nothing to do with wakefulness, or thinking, or her real life. The first few nights she didn't drink anything other than Coke, but one night she had a few beers and had to leave the car and take a cab home. After that, she always taxied out.

The first time she brought a man home was a disaster. He had navy eyes, like a cow, and he did a little cough before he spoke 'Heh-heh' every time. She had met him on the dance-floor. He'd watched her dancing and admired the swish of her red hair and her eyes-closed, unselfconsciousness.

'Heh-heh. So what's your name?' he shouted, sidling in front of her.

'Francine', she bellowed above the music, in the direction of his ear.

'Heh-heh. Frances', he said, 'lovely, lovely. That's my sister's name'.

'Oh', was all she could think of to say.

She only brought him home because he'd kissed her – the first strange mouth she had tasted in twelve years. He was asleep as soon as his head fell to the pillow and she'd shunted him out the door in the morning, relieved to see him go, after staring at the back of his head for the entire night. His small, shorn head that had hogged Roger's pillow.

'Heh-heh, goodbye so', he said, and she nodded and closed the door on his cow-eyes and coughy talk.

'Jesus', she said, leaning into the hallway and wondering at herself.

Francine liked the feel of familiarity. When she woke in her own bed, she could smell her pillow – a comfortable blend of rose face-cream and dirty hair – and her stuff was all around like a safety net: the hulking wardrobe, her ugly dressing-table, the roman blind she'd made herself. She never went back to a man's place, she only felt comfortable as long as she was in her own house. To go back to their's would be giving up her control, while they came to her house she was in charge of each situation. That way, there was no tripping around in the dark searching out a toilet or discarded clothes or the front door, no gasping for a glass of water, but not knowing where to get it. Everything she could possibly want was close by.

Roger nearly caught her only once. He was supposed to be at a conference in Wicklow and Francine arrived back to the house in a taxi with a Frenchman she'd met. She had paid the taxi-driver before she saw Roger's car looming in the driveway and she had to bundle the bewildered Frenchman back into the cab and send him on his way.

'Where in God's name were you until this hour?' Roger barked, hopping into the hall the second she opened the front door.

'Out', Francine pussed, put out by his anger.

'Out?' he said, his voice pitching higher. '*Out?*'

'That's right, Roger. Out, as in *not in*'. She dropped her keys on the hall table, crossed her arms and stared at him.

'Out where?'

'With my friend, Carmel'.

'Carmel? Who the hell is Carmel?'

'Oh just shag off, Roger. You know nothing about me, you're not one bit interested in me, so how would you even know the names of any of my friends?' Francine clumped past him up the stairs and he stood, staring after her.

The next time was better: the man had leonine curls and an easy way. She met him at the bar when she ordered her first drink, he stood there with a light smile patched onto his face. He nodded a hello and they chatted for a bit. They danced together, pressed front-to-front in the dark heat of the club. She brought him home and they talked most of the night about films they both liked and countries they had visited. He was off to Greece for three months, to see what he could see, he promised to send her a postcard from the best island he found there.

She took him in her arms and loved the hot-cold slide of sweat that passed between them, the strange feeling of him moving under her, tucked up inside her. It was dawn before they slept, a wedge of light spreading down the bed through the bottom of the blind, where it didn't quite reach the windowsill. In the morning he drank a mug of hot water, instead of tea, and left the smell of cigarettes in Francine's white kitchen. When it was time for him to go, he kissed her long and hard, standing at the front door, and she opened her eyes half-way through to make sure the neighbours weren't spying. They weren't.

His eyelashes curled up long like a baby's.

Roger found out, of course. She was seen, observed, watched, and the loose mouths in the town couldn't bear to stay shut. He rounded on her in the kitchen one evening, lost the plot completely. He cursed at her, using the kind of words that only the self-styled devout resort to when they're angry. Francine stood and listened to him, marvelling at his filthy vocabulary. She felt like giving him a round of applause when he'd finished. Instead she watched a line of spit careen from the side of his lips, down his chin, into his shirt collar.

'Finished?' she asked, cocking her head like an inquisitive bird. His face reeled up, plum-coloured. 'Guess what, Roger?' she roared, 'there's a person living inside this manky tracksuit'. She plucked madly at her clothes. 'A real live human being, with real live wants and needs'. She slugged her tea, made a meal of it, slurping and staring at him over the rim of the cup.

'Harlot', he spat.

'Oh what's this, the Bible?' She sniggered, 'Harlot!' and slammed down her tea-cup.

'Well you'd know all about that, wouldn't you, Francine? You know plenty about all things *biblical*'.

They faced one other – the air a snarl between them – then they fell on each other and kissed, like they hadn't kissed in years.

Roger left the next day.

Mick, the man with the Our Lady of Guadalupe tattoo, was the last one she brought home. He had taken her phone number at the nightclub, before she'd brought him home, and after a few days he rang. Francine eyed the phone, thinking it might be someone she didn't want to speak to. She counted eight rings, then snatched up the receiver, before it was too late.

'Francine? It's Mick'.

'Oh, Mick, how are you?'

'I'm grand. Fine. I'm well'. He paused. 'Listen, Francine, I have a bit of a confession to make'. She listened to the hum of the phone-line and wondered what words were going to come across the wires next. 'The thing is, I'm actually not married at all'. He giggled. 'Are you still there?

'Yes, I'm here'. She pushed her toes into the carpet.

'I just thought that *you* were. Married, I mean, that's why I said that. I live at home with my folks'. The wires sang.

'I *was* married once', Francine said, and smiled into the phone.

'I was just wondering, would you like to come out for a spin with me sometime, on my motorbike?'

Francine laughed, her whole body juddered and shook and she held the phone very close to her ear.

'Yes', she said, 'I'd like that very much. Very much'.

THE TRIP

Edward was a raw, open wound of a man; hurt oozed out of every part of him. He never fully met your eyes when he spoke and he had theories about why everyone was wrong about every single thing. Other people annoyed him, including me. My wife Diane hated that I was friendly with him, she christened him the Walking Cadaver, said he looked like a corpse with his blue-pale skin and shadow-gashed cheeks.

It was me who suggested the trip away, I thought it might cheer Edward up. He had been given the flick by yet another woman – the lovely Ursula. He was sitting across from me in the pub, caught up in the middle of a rant about all of her faults.

'She was just so bossy. It was always, "Do this, do that, do the other", in that whingy voice. God, I hated it. And talk about mean! I should've slapped her, you know, on more than one occasion'.

'Ah, Edward, come on –'

'I'll tell you, Patrick, the way she treated me, she deserved a slap'.

'Oh for Christ's sake'. I lowered my pint. 'Hey, maybe we should get out of town for a few days. Away from women and work – a lads' weekend'.

He said he would like that.

It was a woman who checked us in, she remarked that we were the only people staying that night. Edward grunted when she spoke. I looked at him but he turned away. The woman was handsome: square-faced and wide-shouldered, and her thick lipstick feathered into the lines around her mouth. She wore corduroy shoes, those fawn ones that look like slippers – men's shoes. She was at the reception desk, fingering through a magazine, when we arrived. It had just begun to rain. Edward stared at her as if there was something he wanted to say, then he looked out the window. I signed the guest-book, she nodded at me and a small smile lifted the edges of her mouth.

'It must get lonely here', I said.

'Oh, not really, I don't mind'. She shrugged.

'Still, it's quiet, I suppose'.

'It's peaceful. I like that'.

Edward tutted lavishly and pulled his wallet from his coat pocket.

'How much?' he barked.

'For two nights? One hundred and fifty euro'.

Diane and I always joked that butterflies should fly out of Edward's wallet when he opened it, it was such a rare happening. But he paid in advance, shoving the money across the desk without speaking. I let him.

'Have a nice stay', she said, which is what they have to say whether they mean it or not.

We scuttled through the rain to the chalet.

'Silly bitch', Edward muttered as he opened the door. 'Did you see the state of her?'

The room was warm with wood and it smelt fresh. I could hear cows nearby, their lowing as mournful as church music. Rain fell in fat drops against the window. I watched it tumbling down the pane. The group of chalets was in one of those morbid country places where, every day, the hours drag by as wide as elastic. I looked around at the cosiness of the room and felt as lonely as an owl. I wondered if Diane was missing me.

I put on a happy voice. 'So, will we go and find a pub?'

'H*mmm*, I don't know, I'm pretty tired'.

'Well, I'll go and ask the woman at reception what there is to do around here at night'.

Edward sighed. I let myself out and ran through the rain, my jacket hoiked over my head. I clinked open the reception door. The woman had her back to me and I could see she was sipping from a mug, still tossing at the pages of her magazine. The radio hummed quietly; I coughed.

'Oh, you gave me a fright'. She turned, her hand at her throat, and laughed.

'I'm sorry'. She stood, looking confused; her lipstick had been re-done in a violent peach colour. 'I'm interrupting your tea break'.

'What can I do for you?' Her voice was slow and sad.

'I wanted to find out where we could go for something to eat'. She leaned on the desk, rolling her chest onto her arms, and I thought how fragile she looked for such a large woman. 'Maybe a pub or a restaurant'. She looked at me as if I wasn't there. 'It's a nasty night'. I waved at the rain-streaked window.

'Yes, nasty'. She scratched at a mole on her cheek, it was a familiar, absent movement, one she turned to all the time I imagined. 'There's a pub about a mile from here, they do toasted sandwiches, soup, that sort of thing. Turn right at the gate'.

'Thanks'. I smiled at her, then held the smile a bit too long and wondered if she'd think I was leering. Her eyes clicked onto mine.

'You have a beautiful face', she said quietly, 'honest'.

I felt my neck get hot. 'Oh, thanks'. I blustered out through the door. 'Good God', I mumbled to myself, jumping over the puddles on the pathway.

'I suppose you rang Diane', Edward said. He lay on his bed, staring at the ceiling. 'Kissy, kissy'.

'No, actually, I was too busy being propositioned by the receptionist'. I giggled and Edward snorted, pulling the sound down through his nose into his throat.

'That old cow? I'll tell you what she needs –'

'Oh shut up, there's nothing wrong with her. She may spend a little too much time on her own, but that's all. Come on, there's a pub down the road'.

Edward plucked at his jumper with his fingers, his face was waxy. Diane was right: he did look like a dead body – stuck with an ugly frown that no undertaker could remove.

'I just can't figure out what went wrong with Ursula, you know, it was all going fine as far as I was concerned'. He sighed.

I sat down on my bed and gripped the spongy quilt between my fists, so that I wouldn't speak. I wanted to say, 'Maybe it was your constant negativity that made her leave you; your cynicism. Maybe she got fed up with your meanness, sick of paying for everything when you went out. Maybe she was embarrassed by the ratty jumpers you wear and the stink of damp that trails behind you like a huge pair of wings'. But I tongued the sentence aside.

'I think I'll stay here', he said, rolling into the covers. 'Have a little sleep'.

'Jesus, Edward, why did we bother coming away at all if you're just going to lie there sleeping and moaning? Lighten up, will you?'

He sat up.

'It's alright for you, Patrick, with your cosy happily-married existence and your great job. You act as if you're so perfect all the time. Patrick and Diane, Mr and Mrs Perfection, so bloody superior they don't even pick their noses. Well, you're not perfect you know'. He stared past me, at some point beyond my head, his breath toppling through his nose in short blasts.

'You're your own worst enemy, Edward, do you know that?' I got up and stalked out through the door.

He followed me to the pub. I was on my second pint, lazily watching a soccer match on the telly when he came in, looking like an overgrown boy in his rain jacket. He stayed by the door, getting in people's way, looking for me. I could see that the wet had seeped through to his jumper and he was pissed off. I raised my glass and he came over.

'Silly fucker', he said, 'why did you run off like that?' He called for a pint.

'I'll have another, Edward', I said. 'If you please'.

'Shut up', he said, and ordered a pint for me.

We ended up playing darts with two local girls, Bea and Mary. I was useless at it, but Edward was surprisingly – and smugly – skilled. The girls flirted mightily and made us buy their drinks. Edward seemed to be enjoying himself. I slipped my arm around Bea's waist, the one who'd clung closest to me; she was puddingy, beautiful.

'Now, now', Edward said, 'less of that, Patrick, don't forget you're spoken for, a *married* man'. He waggled his finger and grinned; his smiles didn't meet his eyes.

'Jesus, Eddie, you really know how to kill a mood', Bea said, and myself and the girls laughed. Edward had a pint to his mouth, he drew it away.

'Oh that's right, laugh at me. Laugh at poor stupid Edward. Edward the mood killer'. He slammed his glass down. 'You're all the same, do you know that?'

'Who are all the same?' Mary asked.

'Women'.

'Edward', I said.

'Woooooo ...', Mary teased, 'we're all the same are we? And what's that supposed to mean?' She was smiling.

'Bloody bitches', he spat, grabbed his jacket and left the pub. The door flung closed.

'Fuck it, I quite fancied him', Mary said, and hiccupped loudly. She shrugged, raised her glass to me and took a slurp of her drink. 'Oh well'.

I got up to go after him.

'Ah don't', Bea said, hanging onto my arm.

'I'm supposed to be cheering him up this week-end'.

'Stay with us, don't mind him'.

I said I would finish my pint, but then I'd have to go, I sank it quickly. Bea dragged me outside and we kissed under a wall-lamp behind the pub. We were both drunk and we toppled over onto some crates that were stacked alongside the wall. We laughed and kissed again, I held her and smelt the tang of a fruity shampoo from her hair, while she smoked a fag over my shoulder.

'Your friend's a bit weird, is he?' she said.

'Ah, he's alright'.

We kissed some more, probing each other's mouths with hot tongues, and then I sent her back inside, saying I would see her the next night. I jogged back along the dark road. By the time I got back I was soaked, so I took a scalding shower, opened a bottle of whiskey and switched on the telly. The next thing I remember is waking to find the light blaring and Edward sitting on my bed. He was talking to himself.

'You're back', I said, struggling through the pain of an early hangover. I squinted and rubbed at my eyes. He was grunting like a pig. I sat up and stared: he was covered in blood. Smears of red chunnelled down his face and his hands were filthy with it. I sprang forward. 'Jesus, Edward, what happened to you?'

He looked at me. 'I didn't mean it'. He started shuddering and crying, girlish little sobs.

'Edward, just tell me what you're talking about'. I put my hand on his shoulder.

He got up and gestured for me to follow. I pulled my clothes on, he opened the door and walked out into the rain. I followed him to the reception, he stood to one side and pointed at the door. I backed up to it, afraid to let him out of my sight, and went in. The radio was thrumming mood-music.

'Hello?' I called, creeping towards the desk, scanning the room. I couldn't see the receptionist. My body thundered. 'Hello, is anybody here?' I saw her feet, still safe inside the corduroy shoes, sticking out from behind the desk. 'Oh Christ'.

I crouched down and tried to turn her over, to see her face. I lifted her hand, it was warm and butter-soft, it fell to the floor when I let go. I pulled at her side until she flopped onto her back. My breathing strangled me, I cried out and fell backwards. Her face was gone: left in its place was a raw, bloody mush. I heard the door click shut, Edward stood over me.

'She annoyed me', he said. 'They all annoy me'.

Up Up Up

I watched a black-as-tar crow mincing like a rock-star on the path in front of us. He jumped forward two steps, then back, cocked his head, and leapt to the side. I smiled. My bumbones were numb from sitting on the bench and Dara had been talking for ages, his voice pitching and keeling, the more he tried to convince.

'He's putting on a show for us'. I looked at Dara, he made a face – I'd cut across him.

'What?' he said.

'The crow'. I pointed. 'He's dancing. Probably just looking for food'.

'Brenda, are you even listening to me?' He said it quietly, stared at his hands.

'Did you know the Irish word for crow is *préachán*? It's a great word, isn't it? *Préachán*'. I drew the sound of it out over my tongue. 'It sounds exactly like what a crow sounds like. It's onomatopoeic'. I was babbling. I glanced at Dara again. 'Better then caw-caw-caw, anyway'.

The bird bounced backwards, barked from its throat a couple of times, flicked a last look at us and flew off. I gazed down over the park: at the people walking dogs, at the mammies with their buggy-bound babies.

'Well?' he said.

'I'm not sure about it. It's a bit weird'. I took his arm, rubbed it through his coat with my gloved hand. 'What's it they call it – "a mercy fuck"?'

'Yeah, I suppose so. Look, you don't have to do it. I just thought, you know, like I said, you already know each other and Philip needs it, and you're great, you'd be nice to him … well, anyway, think about it'. He pulled me to him and cupped my chin in his hands. 'I love you, Brenda, you know?' He kissed me, a little kiss. We stood up, linked arms and walked down along the path. 'Philip thinks you're a ride – did I mention that already?'

I thumped him on the chest and laughed. 'I'll think about the whole thing. Look, don't mention it again until I've made a decision. I'll let you know'.

Philip's illness fell on him. One day he was alright, the next he had multiple sclerosis. None of us could believe it. We tried to treat him the same as ever before – we slagged him about his lack of a girlfriend, his clumpy hair, his love of Johnny Cash and, later, about the blackthorn walking-stick his uncle gave him to help him get around. His endless tiredness. As his legs weakened, we wheeled him everywhere: to the pub, to gigs, into town. We accused him of being lazy. It was hard watching his muscles freeze up. Hardest of all for him.

Philip was given a wheelchair-friendly flat in a small housing-estate, and an independent living allowance, and he got on with life. I loved this new place: the ramps, the low-level furniture, the wide spaciousness of it. The flat had a dirty-sweet, unlived-in smell, though, that swarmed like the stench over a rubbish dump. It seemed as if the air in the rooms didn't circulate properly because it wasn't moved through enough. But it was a clean-walled, bright space and I liked going there.

I sat in a tub chair, my hands bunched around a mug of tea. Philip sat opposite me in his wheelchair, silent as a painting, looking out the window. Heavy rain had made a turlough of the field below the housing-estate and seagulls were scattered across it like paper boats. We watched them lift and fall on the water, their heads held high.

'It's like being in the middle of the country here', I said.

'Apart from the traffic-noise from the motorway. And the pylons'. His words had started to slur more and more, but I could always understand him.

'And the ambulance sirens and the wailing ice-cream van'. I thought for a minute. 'The mad dogs. The kids'.

'And the junkies, don't forget them. The dealers. Where would we be without our local, friendly, drug lord?' Philip sipped his tea. 'Yeah, it's an idyll alright'. We looked at each other and laughed.

'I brought my camera', I said, reaching into my bag. 'Your Ma asked me to take a few photos of you. For the mantelpiece'.

'For my memorial card, more like'. He smiled. 'Go on, then. But you'd better do something with my hair'.

I left the camera down and wet my hands at the sink. I ran my fingers over Philip's hair, then through it, pulling it into shape. It felt springy and I watched the water change its colour from dirty-blonde to sedge brown.

'That's a bit better', I said, and stood back to look at him.

'Only a bit?'

'I'm using black and white film – you'll look totally gorgeous, in spite of yourself'. I took his tea-cup away and put the camera to my eye. 'There'll be two flashes, Phil, just keep looking at me'.

'I'll try'. He giggled through the side of his mouth, not wanting to look up. 'God, I hate getting my photo taken'.

I took several shots of his face, each one from a different angle. He smiled, then looked serious, then looked out the window. After a while, he seemed to forget about me. I dipped the camera and started to shoot his hands where they lay in his lap. The light from the window made shadows under his wrists and fingers. When I zoomed in, I could see the pores, the hairs, the moles decorating his skin. He had beautiful hands.

'So, I hear you want to fuck me?' I smiled as I said it – the viewfinder still to my eye – but my stomach was hopping.

'What? No, I …' He dropped his chin to his chest, I could see a line of pink scalp through his hair. It made me imagine him as a baby, in his mother's arms.

'It's OK, Philip, Dara told me about your conversation'. I leaned towards him. 'I don't mind, I'm flattered'.

'It was his idea. I mean, *you* were his idea. I just wanted anybody, you know, so that I wouldn't die without ever having …'

He looked away. I put down my camera, onto the floor, and knelt in front of him. I placed my hands over his. 'Don't talk about dying'.

'It's going to happen, Brenda. I have to face it. We all do'.

I laid my cheek against his knees and pushed his hands into my hair. 'Let me know when you're ready, Phil, and I'll be here'.

Dara held me hard that night, his skin close on my skin, the length of his body tight to mine. He breathed in my ear, told me he'd love me forever, called me his gorgeous girl. I savoured his weight pressing down on me, as always, and the slide of our mixed sweat. I licked his ear-lobes, bit them lightly, pressed my hands into the drift of hair along the small of his back, and kissed the mushroom-cloud shapes left on his arm from childhood vaccinations. We bucked together, called each other's names, and he stayed on top of me afterwards for a long time, his cock lying wet and soft inside me, like a flower.

'You don't have to go through with it, Bren, you know? This thing with Philip'.

Dara's mouth was on my neck, making a muffle of his words. I levered his body away from mine, by pushing his chest up, and slid out from under him. I rolled to face him.

'It was your idea'.

'Well, I've changed my mind. We'll think of someone else for him'.

I leaned over, trying to see his face in the grey light. 'Dara, it's too late, I've told Philip I'll go ahead with it'.

'I'll tell him you've changed your mind'.

'But I haven't'. I stroked his cheek. 'You have'.

He stared at me. 'Oh, I see. I get it. You actually *want* to have sex with him'. He turned to the wall, dragging most of the quilt with him. I poked his back with a fingernail.

'Turn around. Turn around to me, Dara'. He wouldn't. I pulled at his arm, kissed the tattoo on his shoulder, tugged at the sweat-soaked ends of his hair. 'I don't particularly want to have sex with Philip'. I paused. 'But he's our friend'. He shrugged my hand off his skin. 'Dara. *Dara*. Oh, just fuck off then. It seems to have slipped your mind that you were the one who came up with this. Not me'. I turned my back to his and we lay, spine to cold spine.

Philip's mouth tasted different to Dara's: sweeter, softer, less urgent. I hadn't been expecting to like his kisses. We'd decided to have a practice run – to ease the pressure on both of us – so that if it went wrong, we knew we could try again. He was in bed when I arrived. I let myself in with the key he'd had cut and called out that it was only me.

I could tell, when I slid in beside him, that his underwear was new – I could see loose, same-colour threads clinging to the fabric. I was touched. I'd worn a white vest and knickers set – nothing too clingy or obvious – I didn't want to give him a fright. Philip lay on his back and I put my hand onto his bare stomach. He shivered.

'Am I cold?'

'No, not really'.

I cuddled in closer to him, laid my head on his chest. I liked the heft of him. Dara was slim, almost slight, and it was nice to feel Philip's bulk under my arms.

'Love the hairy chest, mister. What a man!'

He laughed, hugged me close to him and we kissed, deep and long.

'Is this OK?' he asked, and I said that it was. I touched his cheeks and told him that we didn't have to do anything this time, we'd take it as slow as he liked. The heat of his skin was heating mine and I leaned in and kissed him again, playing my tongue over his lips. 'This feels mad', he said, his nose touching mine, his hands wrapped into my hair.

'I know. But it's kind of comfortable too. Strangely so'.

'I was just thinking the same thing', he whispered.

I breathed deep on Philip's smell – a mix of damp skin and something like camomile – and slid my tongue slowly over his. My hands caressed his skin, up and down the length of his body, over his bum. His breathing changed. I asked him if he was alright and when he nodded, I peeled back his boxer-shorts and straddled him, he moaned from somewhere far down inside and I started to move.

I had collected the photographs of Philip from the developers on the way home. I sat at the kitchen table to open the package, I wanted to arrange them into an album for his mother. I heard a clicking noise and looked up: a magpie was doing a crazy polka on the windowsill outside. I watched it jump in taut circles – it seemed to be searching for something. I saluted it and said, 'Good day, good day Mr Magpie', to keep away the bad luck it might bring. I took the photos from their pack. The door opened, Dara came in and stood at the kitchen counter, smoking.

'I didn't realise you were going to stay the whole night'.

'Oh'. I looked past him, not meeting his eyes. I noticed, for the first time, that the wall behind him was like a sweep of cellulited skin: the pale paint mottled and puckered all over. I yawned.

'Tired?' He flicked his ash into a yogurt pot.

'No, just hungry. Smoke that in the garden, will you, Dara?' He was staring at me.

'So, how did it go?'

'I'm not discussing it'. I got up and opened the fridge, then looked up at him. 'As agreed'.

'Suit yourself'.

Dara began to clip his nails with his teeth, spitting the leavings into the air; his jumper was sprigged with dandruff. I looked at him and sighed.

'You could do with a shower, sweetheart', I said, putting my hand on his belly and rubbing it.

'I'm sure you could do with one yourself'.

Finishing his smoke, he rinsed the smelly fag-end under the tap before throwing it into the sink. He shrugged into his coat and left.

The magpie jittered and hopped outside and I stared at it, then back down at the photos on the table. I spread them out and flicked through them, then stacked them in a thick heap in front of me. None of the ones of Philip's face had come out properly: they were fogged and shaky. In every picture, he looked like a moving ghost, his features a surreal blur. The ones of his hands were perfect, though: sharp, with the shadows stark and deep. I spent ages peering closely at them and trailing my fingers over his.

PASCHA'S WAR

Pascha had seen a war. He had lost his mother to it – the mother whose gold teeth shone darkly between her lips when she smiled, and who had suckled him long after he could run about with the other boys. She was sliced across the belly by a man with small hands and tightly curled hair; he laughed when the pain made her throat gurgle. Pascha knelt beside her in the roadway and tried to press the wound shut with his fingers, his schoolbooks and pencils scattered in the dust.

Like many of those who witness war, he didn't want to talk about the things he had seen. It clouded him and made his every movement serious. When Tom held him at night, his body crooked around Pascha's, he could sense the relief that sleep gave him: the unbending of the limbs, the quietening of his face. Tom would kiss him lightly on the skin, to keep him safe, and if he moved away at all, Pascha followed him across the bed. Lately, Pascha had started to talk about going back; he mentioned leaving Prague for a little while.

They sat opposite each other in a basement café on Borivojova. Pascha watched the ankles of the passing pedestrians through a slit of window set high on the wall, while Tom scrabbled at his beard with his fingernails.

'I want to see the place again', he said, knowing by Tom that he didn't want him to go. 'I still have family there, friends'.

'What's the point in looking backwards? The past is the past. Better to leave it there'.

'It's different for you. You live here, where you belong, I haven't had that in so long, I forget what it feels like'.

'You belong here. With me', Tom said, holding out his hand to the younger man. 'It's not possible to go back'.

'Maybe'. Pascha gave Tom his hand and let him kiss his fingers, one at a time.

'Why don't we take a holiday instead? We could go to Italy, Sardinia, if you like'.

'I don't need another holiday'.

'Come on, finish your beer. I have something I want to show you', Tom said.

He stood and Pascha followed him up the stairs, his nose nearly touching the seat of Tom's trousers, which were taut across the bulk of his behind. He smiled and tapped him on the buttocks, Tom turned and winked at him. After the climb to the street, Tom stopped at the top of the steps and puffed elaborately through his nose, then breathed in the warm air. They headed down the grass-caked cobblestones to the studio, passing an ancient woman who bawled into a mobile phone while dragging a tatty lapdog on a lead.

Tom fussed with the keys until, as usual, Pascha took them from him and unlocked the door.

'My old eyes', Tom said.

'There's nothing wrong with your eyes'.

Pascha fiddled with the light switch until it obliged and threw himself across the room, onto the velvet sofa. Tom told him not to dare look until he had the painting in position. He lifted it onto an easel, stood back and appraised it for a moment before saying, 'Now, it's ready'.

Pascha turned to face the canvas. Like much of Tom's work, it was a large abstract of a head, Picasso-esque in its vulgar beauty. The painting showed a woman – in a chaos of yellow and blue brushstrokes – her head thrown back in pain, or possibly lust. She held a flower to her face between pinched fingers and her mouth was crowded with ochre teeth.

'It's your Mama', Tom said.

'I know'.

The square gable-end of the house faced Pascha, its former whiteness veined with green mildew. The garden was a rutted patch of muck. He dropped his rucksack in the road and rolled his shoulders, first backwards then forwards, squinting at the house to see what it might tell him. He moved around in front of it and saw a red cloth flapping in the front window, he could hear the thrum of a transistor radio from inside, playing a German waltz. The front door was ajar and he knocked on it before pushing it wide. Two people lay under a huddle of sheets on the bed in the corner. His grandmother, half the size of her former self, sat up in the bed and stared at him, her dark eyes blank.

'Grandma', Pascha said, and she held out her arms.

He ran forward, knelt by the low bed and hugged her, she was as wizened as a rotten apple and her lightness in his arms scared him. The other person in the bed moved and he saw that it was his uncle Aslanbek – or an old-man version of him, at least. Pascha smiled and began to greet him. Aslanbek hoisted himself up onto his elbows and started to yelp, Pascha backed away. His uncle shut his eyes, he continued to yap and bark like a lost dog, until his mother took hold of his chin and held a hand-mirror in front of his face. She pinched and pulled at Aslanbek's cheeks until he focussed on his reflection and, once he recognised himself, the yelping stopped. He lay down again and turned to the wall.

'This is how it is', Pascha's grandmother said, swinging her legs onto the mud-packed floor.

They sat together at the table under the window and she asked him about life in the Czech Republic. She wanted to know if there were killings there, if people disappeared, if it was near America, if the food was wholesome. She pulled a tiny square of cardboard back and forth between her fingers, all the time she spoke. Pascha looked around the room – at the candle stubs, the slop-bucket, the chipped crockery – and tried not to let in the smells of damp, piss and boiled cabbage that clung to the air.

'Your uncle Ivan is missing', his grandmother said, after a long silence. 'Aslanbek went looking for him – he hadn't come home from the pasture'.

'When?'

'Five months ago. When Aslanbek got there, the cattle were roaming free. Ivan's shoes were left side-by-side on a hillock'.

'He won't be coming back then'.

'No, he won't ever be coming back'. She sighed and dropped her chin to her chest. 'I lost your mother. Then Ivan. Now Aslanbek is gone from me, too'. She waved towards the bed. 'He's here, but he's not here'.

'I'll give you money, Grandma. I have plenty'.

'Yes, yes. I will buy nice food, mutton. And batteries for my radio. You are a good boy, Pascha'. She smiled, showing her gums. 'You are married now, yes?'

'No, Grandma, I'm not married'.

'Oh well, in time, in time'. She rubbed his hands. 'But don't bring her back here, whenever you find her. She'll only end up a widow, like every other woman in Chechnya'.

The Vltava was low the evening they walked along its banks, on the way to the opening of Tom's exhibition. They stopped to watch the carp climbing over each other in the water and to let the river-stink assault their noses. Pascha pointed to a wheelchair that was disabled in the silt, the swing of its seat turned ash-grey from being immersed in the river. Tom indicated four footballs floating together and complained of the waste and the pollution. He slipped his arm around Pascha and squeezed him.

'Are you OK?'

'I'm fine. You?'

'Nervous'. Tom grimaced, then smiled.

They walked on towards The Bedroom Gallery, where the opening was to take place. The owner, Spy, met them at the door, carrying a tray of champagne glasses. Pascha hadn't met her before and was embarrassed when she shouted a welcome and kissed him on the mouth. Tom embraced her and grabbed some champagne. He moved off, stopping here and there among the crowd, chatting to well-wishers, hoping to entice people to buy some paintings.

Pascha sidled from portrait to portrait, each one a figure from his childhood. Tom had adapted them from a few blotchy, blurred Polaroids that Pascha had allowed him to use. There was Mama, open-mouthed, screaming silently. Here was Grandma, her headscarf a startling green she would never wear in real life. There was Ludmilla, smiling happily, long before the days when she was forced to beat Murat, her brother, to death with a stick by Russian soldiers; years before she was gang-raped. There were Ivan and Aslanbek, arms around each others' shoulders, their brotherly gaze comically askew.

And here was Pascha himself – a life-sized nude – coy and solemn, his body a blend of regal purples. Pascha felt his neck grow hot, he hadn't seen this painting before, and, though he loved Tom and knew he was loved in return, he felt suddenly betrayed. He stood in front of the portrait for a few minutes, taking in the raw, cold feel of it. When he was sure no one was looking, he slipped out through the gallery's front door, into the warm Žižkov night.

Ludmilla smiled up at him, her lean hands holding his face. Pascha was nervous, afraid nothing would work as it should.

'It's alright', she whispered, and lifted her pelvis to guide him in. 'There', she sighed and Pascha gasped. They moved together, slowly at first, gathering a rhythm. Ludmilla's cheeks grew pink and Pascha had to pull his eyes away from her face, so that he could concentrate. She was as pretty as a plastic doll – all the boys loved her – and she was Pascha's friend. They had agreed to this union, to get it over and done with for both of them.

Ludmilla asked him to kiss her and he lowered his lips to her mouth, tasted her soft tongue. He felt the wind on his backside and heard some of the smaller children playing war-games, while the real guns blared in the distance. His body began to buck and jerk in a way he couldn't stop, then he cried out and collapsed onto Ludmilla's small frame. She kissed his ear and giggled, and he lay on top of her for a short while, smelling the fustiness of her hair. Then Pascha dragged her off the ground by the arm and helped her to fix her clothes, he pulled up his shorts with his free hand. They ran back to the village together, laughing.

'When Murat tried to run away, the soldiers caught him – two of them. They dragged him back to where the rest of the children stood and they tied his hands behind his back. They made the others hit Murat with sticks, they shouted at them. Ludmilla refused, she told them he was her brother. They said they were going to shoot her, they put a gun on her neck'. Pascha stopped and put his fingers to a spot below his ear. 'Murat screamed at her, "Why are you doing this to me, why?"'. He was crying, Ludmilla was crying, she felt sick'. Pascha's face crumpled. 'When he was dead, the soldiers made them smear his blood on their arms and faces'. He sighed. 'She dreamt about him every night, each time the same thing: Murat told her she had killed him for nothing, her own brother. She would cry and hold out her hand to him, but he always turned away'.

Tom held Pascha in his arms. 'Where is she now?'

'Back there, taking care of her mother. Fighting'. He looked up into Tom's eyes. 'And I am here'.

'Yes, you're here. With me', he kissed Pascha's nose, 'where you belong'.

LOVEDAY

It was by accident that I met Jack Loveday. I had dipped into the art gallery to escape a rain shower – one of those hot, sulphurous ones that means thunder is on its way – and got sucked into the hush and reverence of the place by its smell: it was ancient and fresh at the same time. I wandered through the front atrium, past rows of brooding stained-glass panels, and into the first exhibition room. My trench-coat was soaked, so I took it off and shook it out, it spluttered plump raindrops onto the parquet floor. Some of the drops hit Loveday's shoes.

'Oops-a-daisy'. He laughed and I looked at him. Something about his face was so chirpy that I laughed too.

'Sorry, I didn't mean to splash you. It's lashing out there'.

'It's OK', he said, 'but I think you need one of those'.

He pointed at the painting in front of him and I turned to look at it. The picture was big, thick with people under a jumble of pigeon-back-blue umbrellas. In the foreground, a hatless woman carrying a bandbox gazed out at us, and a little girl stood coyly by.

'Oh, you mean an umbrella? I'll be fine without one, it's only a shower'.

I squinted at the name-card on the wall: Auguste Renoir, *Les Parapluies*. I smiled at the man and moved off. He stayed where he was, looking at the painting. I glanced back and watched him swinging on his heels and smiling to himself.

He was older, a bit tweedy looking, but I liked his friendly face and soft-looking hair.

The gallery was small and the rooms were in layers, each one stacked behind the last, like a Mayan temple laid out on its back. I moved past the exhibits and got caught up in the speed of the changes: one set of paintings was all languid, light-dappled Breton landscapes, the next was abstracts, exploding their colours and textures across the walls. I stopped in front of a canvas that held a huge fragmented red circle, trying to decide if I liked it or not.

'We meet again'. He was at my elbow and, when I turned to him, his face was almost touching mine. For whatever reason, I didn't want to pull back. 'What's your name?'

'Hannah'. I blushed. 'Yours?'

'Loveday. Jack Loveday. Have some tea with me, Hannah'.

I nodded and we walked back through the gallery's rooms to the table-cluttered café. At the counter, he put his hand on my waist and I slipped my arm around him. My fingers landed on the comforting wad of pudge over his trouser waistband.

It started from there. He took me back to his house that afternoon, he petted my hands on the bus, the palms and the backs, and we delivered slow smiles back and forth to each other. His place was near the coast – a tall Georgian house filled with bachelor's things: there were piles of newspapers and books everywhere, a clatter of uncomfortable chairs, an old stereo. A fruity-grassy smell, like olive oil, hung over everything. We sat side by side on a collapsing sofa and I curled my hands through the ends of his hair while he kissed my neck. Through the sash-window I watched streaks of sunlight probe through storm clouds and crawl across the floor to my feet.

'Would you like to go upstairs?' Loveday whispered into my collar, and I said that I would.

He took my hand and led me up two flights; the stairwell was hung with rows of prints and photographs and watercolours, in gilt and black frames. I didn't stop to look at them, but followed him up the stairs. A large iron bed stood in his room, the quilt cascading over the edge.

'It's a bit messy', he said, bending to lift the ends of the covers out of the rolls of hairy dust that were scattered around the bed like rain-clouds.

I stopped his effort at tidying, took his face in my hands and kissed him deeply, pushing my tongue between his teeth. He kissed me back, the heat of his mouth sent ripples to my stomach. Loveday slipped his hands inside my clothes and unhooked my bra, I pulled my shirt off and my breasts swung free. He lifted and held and kissed them in turn. We undressed quickly – only glancing at each other's nakedness – and lay down together.

It was my first time in a long time. I was conscious of the pouch of my stomach and the wispy hair under my arms that I'd stopped bothering to shave. While he lapped at the skin around my throat, I tried to figure out how it was I felt so comfortable lying naked in his bed on a wet Saturday afternoon. He moved down my body, stroking my sides with his fingers, stopping to kiss my nipples.

'You're beautiful', I said to him, and he lifted his face to me and smiled. I put my index fingers into the hollows at the top of each of his cheeks, then slipped my hands around his neck and lay back against the pillow.

We met at Loveday's house every Saturday after that. I would take the bus or the train and stroll to his place, watching the waves churning on the water in the harbour and the yachts pushing over the sea like toys in a pond. He would open the front door with a smile and hold it wide to let me in. We always talked a little about our during-the-week lives: I told him about the people I worked with in the office, made them all sound a bit more interesting and flirty than they actually were. Loveday would nod and smile in his avuncular way, rubbing my hand all the time, and remember things I'd said about this one or that one. He would ask me if I'd been to the theatre or a film since, then talk a little about meetings he'd had, or places he had been. He called me his sweetheart. We sat together on the sofa facing the window, reading the papers and drinking tea, until we climbed the picture-crowded stairs to his room.

In Loveday's bed we grew hot together, moving across, over and around each other, kissing and tasting and thrusting through hours, until we were sleepy. He was a slow-moving lover, gentle and generous, and I responded to him, forgetting any shyness. I loved to watch his chest tighten as he moved over me, the pull of muscle under skin. I tracked the changes in his face and kissed him everywhere I could reach – face, chest, shoulders, arms. His hands would rub and coax me and he'd watch my face, ask me if he was doing OK, and smile when I said he was. We would sleep in snatches and wake up to touch and play with each others bodies again. I loved the damp-sweet smell of his skin, the hot taste of his tongue on mine.

We sometimes met in town on a Sunday afternoon. We inspected the statues in St Stephen's Green, had coffee and buttery biscuits in hotel foyers, and often ended up back at the Municipal Gallery.

'She reminds me of you, you know'. We were standing in front of *Les Parapluies*.

'Because this is where we first met?' I asked, slipping my hand through the crook of his elbow.

'Well, yes, I suppose, but you look like her too. The same sloe eyes, the superior look'.

'What?' I poked his belly with my finger. 'What are you on about?'

'I don't know, just look at the way she carries herself. She's a hat-maker but she acts like a princess; her head is thrown back'.

'Why shouldn't she act like a princess?' I laughed. 'And what are you saying about *me* – that I'm snooty-looking?'

Loveday laughed and kissed my cheek. 'Look at how flustered you get. I love it'. He held me by the shoulder and we lingered in front of the painting. 'Renoir liked blue – he had a gift with it. But it never made his work dark or sombre, like you might expect'.

'Maybe he was in love with blue'.

'Maybe', Loveday said, taking my face in his hands and kissing my mouth. 'Come on – we need some tea'.

It was a tepid autumn Saturday, when we lay wrapped together in Loveday's bed, half-in half-out of sleep, that his telephone rang. It was such an unfamiliar noise in his house that my eyelids jerked wide and I lay rigid for a moment, not knowing what bed I was in, or who lay spooned around me. Loveday was already lifting the receiver by the time I came back to myself and knew where I was.

'Hello'. His voice became deep and dull, like a civil servant's. I could hear a babble at the other end of the phone-line. 'Margaret, is that you?' I rolled into the quilt and listened, hearing the lilt of concern in his voice. 'Calm down, sweetheart, and start again. Deep breaths, now, come on, I'm listening'.

I listened to the voice on the line – it sounded jerky and tough – but I couldn't make out the words. He soothed and cajoled, asked if she had been drinking, said he would come straight over. The other voice grew louder but Loveday stayed calm and repeated that he would be with her soon. He told her to go and lie down until he got there. He plopped the receiver back and turned to me, he didn't say anything but ran his hand over the mound of my belly and down my inner thigh.

'I have to go out for a while, Hannah, you're welcome to stay'.

He sighed and pushed his hand over his face. I waited for him to tell me where he was going and who the woman on the phone was, but he was already lurching out of the bed and reaching for his clothes. A sting wound its way into my chest.

'Who was that?'

He continued to dress himself, his back to me, and I watched his flesh roll as he bent and moved, lifting his legs one at a time into his trousers. I wanted him to touch me.

'That was Margaret'. He buckled his belt, knelt on the floor by the bed and took my hand; he kissed it and looked into my eyes. 'My daughter'.

'Oh'. It was all that came out of me. His daughter. 'I didn't know you were married'.

Loveday laughed, the kind of laugh parents use with a child who has said something naïve.

'You don't need to be married to make babies, sweetheart'. He tapped me on the nose with his finger. I blushed, furious with him for making fun of me. 'Give me a couple of hours and I'll be back in there beside you'.

He blew a kiss at me before leaving the room, I listened to him trot down the stairs and held my breath for the click of the front-door. Then I lay, marooned in the quiet of his bed, and let scalding tears slide from my eyes into my ears. I got up quickly, tussled into my clothes and left.

The following Friday I took the train home to visit my mother. She was happily retired in a tiny bungalow on the edge of the town. The farm I'd grown up on was too far out now, she preferred the movement of neighbours around her. Mammy was glad to see me, full of the news of the parish: births, deaths, small scandals. She hinted at her own death, then looked at me slyly and we both laughed. My mother was – and is – robust. She asked, as usual, about my love life.

'Oh, there's no one special', I said.

'Hmm', she said, staring at me above the rim of her mug. '"No one special", she says'.

'Oh shut up, Mammy'.

I made a curry for her, she liked it and sat spooning rice into her mouth long after I'd finished eating.

'Whoever he is, he's put you in bad form'.

I looked at her and said nothing. I couldn't decide whether I'd been childish to leave Loveday's the previous week, or whether I'd been right. Who keeps the fact that they have children a secret? The thought made me wince.

'Oh, I'll get over it'. I fiddled with the oilcloth on the table and looked at the floor.

'Go out to the farm and see Gerard while you're here, he'd love to see you, I'm sure'. She scooped the rice around her plate, following it with her spoon to try to catch the last few grains. 'Now, that was gorgeous', she said, when she'd finished and she smiled at me.

I hadn't spoken to my brother Gerard in months, we weren't close, not since I'd moved to the city. The family always worried about him but, being us, we never really did anything to help. It was as if it would be too embarrassing to offer advice, too presumptuous. Gerard was odd. He still ran the farm in a small way, but he always seemed to choose his own company above anyone else's. I said I'd go to see him the next day, it would pass the time.

The bus left me at the top of the valley. I decided not to ring Gerard for a lift; I'd walk. The breeze cleaned my head after the bus and I welcomed the gravelly road underfoot. The day was misty but I could make out the hump of the mountain beyond the houses and the blanket of dark sky draped above it. It was quiet as I tripped down the road. I knocked on the front door, enjoying the familiar weight of the brass knocker Daddy had put there years before. Gerard answered after a minute or two; he looked empty.

'Do you not have a key?'

I did, it just didn't seem like the house had anything to do with me anymore. I stepped into the hall and breathed in the smells: must, onions and furniture polish. I ran my fingernails along the scratchy striped wallpaper. He walked ahead of me to the kitchen. It struck me that not so much as a handshake had ever passed between us.

'Any news?' I asked.

'No, not a thing'.

Gerard sat by the fire, stooped like an old man, the newspaper in his hand. He looked like Daddy had, not long before he died.

'So', he said, half-smiling, 'how's the Big Smoke treating you?'

I hated when people called Dublin that – it seemed rude and provincial.

'Oh, you know …' I unbuttoned my coat, laid it across the back of a chair.

'Come in beside the fire', Gerard said. 'I'll put the kettle on'.

There was a vague smell of pee in the kitchen and the toffee-coloured walls were sloughing paint.

'This place is a shambles'. Gerard grunted and stared into the fireplace, uncomfortable that I was there. We sat without talking. After drinking my tea, I got up. 'I'm going out for a walk'.

'OK'. He didn't offer to come with me and I was glad. I wanted to do something, other than wonder if Loveday was waiting for me, with the day's papers laid out for us to read, the tea wet in the pot.

I tramped through the lane into the back field, swinging left at the old estate wall. The big house there had been idle for years – I'd romanced as a child that I might live in it someday. It all looked less imposing now, not the mansion I used to call it. The pathways were clogged with mulched leaves. I thought about Loveday as I picked through a tangle of plants, feeling like a giant in a child's game. I hoped he was thinking of me. I thought about the way he said I was shaped like a little girl: bud breasts, ripe belly, the small of my back a concave loop. And I thought of him stroking what he called my 'fig-flesh', how expert his touch was, the way it thrilled me to my core. I loved how he liked to curve around me in bed: his front to my back, my head under his chin and my feet standing on his, as if we might dance. He'd tuck his hand over my stomach and press into the mound of it with his fingers.

In the mornings, I often sat and stared into the mirror at his dressing table, complaining that my eyes were drooped over, old-looking, and that if I didn't dye my hair I'd be known as the Grey Lady. Loveday always told me I was beautiful, knowing that that was what I wanted to hear. He said it like he meant it. I stopped kicking through the weeds, stood and looked back at the old house and over at the mountain. I love him, I thought, and I want to tell him.

Gerard was gone up the top field to the sheep when I got back to the house, I could see him from the lane. I let myself in and went to the phone. Loveday's number rang out. I sat at the table and read the newspaper, thinking I'd try to phone him again in a while. I flicked the paper from front to back. I didn't normally read the death notices, because when I did I always seemed to find someone I knew there – a school-friend's mother or some distant relative of my own – and reading of children's deaths always made me feel sad. But as I turned the page an entry stopped me: 'LOVEDAY Máiréad (Margaret) – October 9 (suddenly), deeply regretted by her loving father, family and friends'. I gripped the paper, read it again to the end and went to the phone.

I trailed my fingers through the crumbs on the blue and white plate, pushing them over the scene that showed a pagoda surrounded by trees. My eyes lifted constantly to the café door. The scone I had eaten was lodged between my throat and stomach. I swallowed hard to try to push it along, looked at the doorway again. Loveday appeared at last, his face tired looking. He smiled when he saw me. I stood and we hugged for a long time, he whispered my name into my hair. I ordered more tea and we sat down together.

'Thanks for meeting me', Loveday said.

'I had to see you', I said. He leant over and kissed my lips. 'Tell me what happened'.

He sighed, rubbed my fingers. 'Margaret was an artist, like Maud, her mother'. He frowned. 'I loved Maud, very much, but she was married, you know, so we couldn't be together. She wouldn't leave her husband. Everyone knew that Margaret was mine – it was the worst kept secret in Ireland'. He paused.

'Go on', I said.

'I was Maud's main dealer: I sold her work all over the world. And later, after Maud had passed away, I became Margaret's'. He paused. 'But as her illness took hold, the quality of her work slid and I couldn't sell it anymore. It just wouldn't sell. Margaret became very angry with me, accused me of sabotaging her career to get back at Tony, Maud's husband. We fell away from each other for a long time. Years'. He hung his head. 'I feel so bad about that now'.

'If she was sick, there was probably very little you could do to help'. I fiddled with my tea-cup.

'I could've tried harder. When she was well, she was magnificent: cutting and funny and big-hearted. But when she was depressed, there was a prison-wall around her'.

I patted his arm. 'Prison-walls are notoriously difficult to break through'. He nodded.

'Margaret changed her name to mine a few years ago, she became a Loveday. I think that got to Tony, but I was touched really, honoured. It was the sort of gesture she was capable of: impulsive and well-meant, but hurtful to some'. He half-smiled and I kissed his cheek.

'Come on, let's walk'. I stood up and held out my hand to him. He looked up at me.

'She killed herself, Hannah'.

'I know, Jack'.

He got up, put his two hands on my waist and thanked me again for coming to see him. I hugged him close and we walked arm-in-arm through the gallery, looking for the shelter of our favourite umbrellas.

RUNT

Mem calls me the runt, she says, 'Oh what a piggy pong', when I'm in the kitchen. Granddaddy says, 'Will you ever stop', to Mem, but she just slints her eyes at me and cuts her throat with one finger. Granddaddy has long teeth that are brown and rough like tree bark, they stick out when he opens his mouth. His cap smells as greasy as his head. Mem calls him the blackguard – even though she's his daughter – but she says it with a twisty smile.

Granddaddy and Mem own me now, I live in the back room with a picture of Elvis and the brown statue of Saint Anthony. The walls are cold and sweaty, and the window is tangled with ivy, so it's always dark. All my clothes are in a trunk and my books and toys are on the floor. My job is to help Granddaddy in the shed and keep out from under Mem's feet. That's important, she doesn't want the likes of me trailing muck through her nice clean house.

The shed is full of things: two black bicycles, a bench covered in tin boxes full of nails and bolts, a fishing net, a motorbike engine, a box of onions, a nudie lady calendar, a smell like old grass, a can of petrol, and mice, mice, mice. We're building shelves for my room but first have to kill the mice, every last fecker of them. They're scruffy: they chew the onions and leave dots of poo all over the bench and floor.

'Why don't we make a big trap with a box and a stick, then we can catch them all at the one time?' I say.

'Hmmm, we'll see. Mice are clever little bastards, maybe we'll just set a few small traps'.

'With cheese?'

'A bit of cheese and a bit of bread rolled together. They love that'. Granddaddy smiles at me. 'Or maybe we should just let Big Tom in?'

Big Tom is Mem's cat and no way does she want him chawing mice, their blood might get on his fur and make him dirty. If she saw him with a mouse she would probably blame me. I shake my head.

Granddaddy and me go in the car to town for the traps: eight for mice and two big silver ones for rats, just to be on the safe side. We stop at the Ball Alley for a pint on the way home. The woman working there calls me a poor craythur and her eyes go all swimmy. She gives me orange and crisps and kisses my head with her lipstick mouth, I hope it's not on my hair. The woman goes back behind the bar and wipes glasses and lights a cigarette, I watch the smoke jetting out of her nose while she talks to Granddaddy and the other men. I sit at a table near the door, by myself. She comes over to me and points out the window, to the trees across the road.

'Can you see the upside-down tree, loveen?' She winks at Granddaddy. I look over at the trees on the other side of the road. They all look right-side-up to me. 'See that one', she says, kneeling beside me and pointing with her skinny finger. 'The roots are where the branches should be. Do you see it?'

I nod, to let her know that I can see the upside-down tree too, because she sees it and she seems happy about it, then she lets out a huge laugh and ruffles my hair.

'The craythur', she says again.

'Come on, boyo', Granddaddy says, lugging his pint, 'time to go'.

Mem is sitting at the table when we get home, her eyes are googly and her nose is red. She has a letter in her hand.

'Bad news?' Mem nods. Tears spill over her eyes onto her cheeks, a line of snot dribbles down her lip. Granddaddy taps her on the shoulder. 'It'll be alright'.

'It won't be alright!' Mem screeches, jumping up. 'I'm bad enough without this'. She balls the letter up and holds it in front of Granddaddy's face. 'Who'll want me now?'

'Now, Mem, now, honey'.

Mem's whole body shakes and she cries and cries, loud like a baby. She plunks back down onto the chair and says, 'What the fuck are you looking at?' to me.

I go into my room and lie on the bed. I can hear muttery talking from the kitchen. Elvis sneers at me with his blubbery lip, so I stick out my tongue at him. I'd love to smack him. I pull a book from the floor and read a bit of it but it's too pukey, so I drop it back on the pile. They're not talking anymore.

'Come on, so'. Granddaddy is standing in the doorway. We walk to the shed, he hands me a greasy paper bag. 'Get cracking'.

I squash bits of cheese around pieces of bread to make small smelly clumps. Granddaddy pushes them into each trap, one at a time, then bends back the hinge and clips it in place.

'Now', he says, when they're all done, and we lay the traps carefully around the shed.

'Why is Mem so upset?'

His long teeth catch his upper lip and bite it, he sighs.

'She's not well'.

'How do you mean? She looks OK'.

'She was at the hospital for some tests and the results are not good'.

'Oh. Like my Mammy'.

'A bit like that. Mem has to have an operation. Here'. He lays his hand across his chest. I look at him and giggle. Granddaddy's hand comes out of nowhere and lands hard on my ear. 'You little bastard, this is no laughing matter'.

My fingers fly to the side of my head, my ear is flaming. I start to whimper and Granddaddy puts out his hand.

'*You're* a bastard', I scream, pushing him away. I run from the shed, back up to the house.

Mem has her blue suit on, her hair is washed and tidy. She is sitting on the side of my bed. I'm still dressed, even my runners are on my feet. Mem is holding the two bits of the statue of Saint Anthony and looking at me. He's broken right across the middle.

'What happened to this?' I put on a puss and eye her. 'The face on you'. Mem wiggles the two halves of the statue and grins. 'It doesn't matter, anyway, it's a horrible old yoke'. She drops Saint Anthony onto the floor, his head breaks off and we both laugh.

'Well, Runty, I've to go to the hospital to get my boob hacked off'.

'I'm sorry, Mem'.

'Ah well, you and me both, kiddo'. She gets up. 'Be a good boy and keep an eye on the old blackguard for me while I'm away, won't you? Make sure him and your Daddy don't drink all the bottles of stout in the press'. I nod and Mem leans forward and kisses my cheek. Her mouth is soft. 'I want flowers when you visit me in the hospital. Decent ones'. She shoves away tears with her hand and sniffs. 'The shed is full of dead bloody mice. They're all to be gone by the time I get back and don't let my Tom anywhere near them'.

'Are you right?' Granddaddy is wearing a suit too. 'Come on, you. Up out of that 'til we get this one off to the hospital and out of our sight at last'.

'Oh, shut up', Mem says, and the three of you walk together out to the car.

We all knew Kate was on the way out, everyone except for Daddy. He kept saying, 'Sure she looks grand, she's fine'. But I could tell she was a goner. Her hair was falling off her head in clumps, like horsehair from a torn mattress, and she wasn't able to get out of the bed to mind the child. Barney was less than useless, as usual. He pissed himself into a corner in Hartigan's and didn't come out of it. Even when she died.

And of course we all knew who'd have to take in the little runt when she popped: me and Daddy. There was no question. I, for one, didn't mind but I knew Daddy was too old to be listening to the goings-on of a child, day in, day out: all that running and leaping and carrying-on. Anyway, within days of the funeral the boy's trunk was packed and he was standing in my kitchen when I got back from the shops. A ferrety little thing with sad eyes. I didn't know what to do with him.

'I'm warning you – don't get in my way', I said. He stared at me. 'I'm not soft like your Mammy was'. He kept on staring, like a sheep. 'Go on so, go outside and play'. He turned and went out. I called after him: 'Wipe your feet before you come back in here, or your Granddaddy will kill you'.

It was that night, in the bath, that I found the lump. I was soaping myself, enjoying the comforting heat of the water, when my fingers landed on it. I pulled my hand away, lay back and scrunched up my eyes. I felt hot and cold. Slowly, I slid my hand up and felt again: it was hard and solid, like a walnut growing under my skin. I couldn't believe it. First Kate and now me, I wasn't even able to cry.

I didn't tell Daddy at first, the silly blackguard would've dropped dead on me. I called to Rita's house the next morning, to see if she could tell me what to do. She was gone to work. I walked down the village and stuck my head into the snug at Hartigan's, hoping she'd have nipped in for a quick one to set her right for the day. All I found was Barney, swaying over his pint like a side of beef in a butcher's shop.

'Mem, Mem, my darling, step in', he said, patting the stool beside him. I didn't go in right away. I held the door in my hand. 'Come in, girl, you're letting out the heat'.

I thunked down beside him. He asked after his little son and ordered a drink for me. I let the heat of the whiskey warm my neck and next thing I knew I was sniffing and bawling, telling Barney about the lump and asking him what the hell was I going to do? I babbled on and on, said I couldn't go and die on the child, just after he'd lost his mother – he needed me. Barney clucked and patted my hand. He gave me his hanky – it was grey with snot, but I used it anyway.

'And what about Daddy?' I wailed. 'Poor, poor Daddy, losing his daughters like flies'.

Barney took me in his arms and pushed my head against the heat of his chest.

'Now, now, Mem', he crooned, 'you're going to be fine. It's all going to be grand. I'm here for you, darling, I'm here'.

He held me for a long time, petting my hair and kissing my ear while I sobbed and hiccuped. Then he told me what to do.

Mem is liverish – she was always that way: even as a baby she found it hard to smile. Life doesn't like to go her way, she says. But, the more you keep on with that kind of talk, the less likely it is that things *will* turn out good. The eels in the river know that.

She was fit to be tied when the young fella was left to us.

'What do I want with a little brat running all over the place?' she roared.

She went on like a mad thing over it: plucked at her hair, effed and blinded, threw things around. Even Big Tom got a belt of her sweeping brush that day, and he's used to molly-coddling. She was upset over Kate dying, I suppose, and over Barney collapsing under his loss. It all got mixed up together.

I was glad to take the little fella in – I'm fond of children – and Kate's boy was always my favourite grandchild. He's so wee: a scrawny pucker of a thing. We couldn't leave him with Barney – he just got pissed and stayed that way, once he realised Kate wasn't going to get better. The child didn't even cry when his mother died, too stunned, I suppose. I found him below in the house, warped with the hunger, so I brought him home to stay with us, sooner rather than later.

It wasn't long after he came to us that Mem found out she was sick herself. I was gutted when she told me. One daughter dying on you is bad enough, but the idea of losing another was too much. We decided not to tell the little fella, at least until we knew what was happening ourselves. Mem was full of courage, as angry and mad about the whole thing as all-get-out, but very brave. She found things for me and the young lad to do, to keep us busy: building shelves, laying traps for the mice, that sort of thing.

I told him about Mem's condition eventually. She was upset when the results from the hospital were bad and he twigged that something was up. Sure, he'd been through it all before. Anyway, didn't the little bugger laugh when I said it – nerves probably – but, God forgive me, I gave him a clip on the ear. He went wild, but we were friends again in no time. It was a hard spell for all of us.

Of course, he's like a new child now. He has Mem wrapped around his little finger – when he can manage to get her attention off Barney. The pair of them spend the days cooing at each other, like love's young dream. It'd make a weaker stomach sick. Myself and the little fella laugh at them.

Her hair fell out after the operation, but she liked wearing the wig. They'd only a blondie one left in the hairdresser's, but Mem said she always thought of herself as a Marilyn Monroe type and snapped it up. She was some sight in that wig, it has to be said: walking down the back lane in her apron and wellies, picking blackberries with the child, her wig-hair sparkling like a halo.

Her own hair is growing back now – wispish and thin – but please God, it'll be back again in all its glory for the wedding. They say a door doesn't close but another one opens. It's been true for us.

One Hare's Foot

This is how I remember it. The clouds above my head are like a frame of ribs and the sun behind them a heart. I lie back in the boat and let the turn of the oars sing to me, while I peer through my eyelids at the passing sky. Rita has insisted on rowing and she grunts with each pull. These are the same noises she makes when I lie over her at night: blunt, throaty sounds. It's one of those complete days, where good feelings pass back and over between us with no effort. I know she'll soon get tired from the weight of the oars, so I watch her for a while and then lie back to rest. The river smells thick: it has that warm, weedy, after-rain smell that clogs the air – a sign of summertime.

It's impossible to think of that day now without a raw thump in my guts.

Rita strains with the oars, concentrating on each dip and draw, throwing her whole body into every movement, the same way she does everything. Her head bows low with each pull, her chin nearly skimming her knees, her eyes closed. She concentrates and swings, swooping and heaving with the oars. I play a tune in my head, based on the rhythm of her rowing and the splosh of the water as we move through it.

She rows the boat straight into a girl's head. The crack of the wood on her skull is as loud as metal on rock. Later I remember that I had heard voices calling out, trying to warn us, but I had taken them for others, like ourselves, playing in the heat, enjoying the sunshine and the river. Rita takes no notice of the people shouting, otherwise she would steer the boat well away from the swimmers. When she does realise what has happened, she drops the oars, throws her head into her lap and holds it there. She moans and wails and rocks.

When I feel the jolt, hear the noise, I pull myself up into the dazzle and the awful careering of the boat. All I can see of Rita is the lattice of her fingers through her black hair. When I look into the water, I see the girl floating away on her back, a liver-coloured slick of blood spreading out from her head. Her mouth is open and her hair swings around her like a crown of seaweed. I stare, gripping onto the sides of the boat, and sweat slides into my eyes. Hordes of people wade into the water, they grab at the girl, trying to stop her from floating away. Rita throws up all over the front of her dress.

The people hated to see the hare on a May morning, especially if it was suckling the milk from the cow. It would often be seen doing that, you know. That brought the worst kind of bad luck. They would have to run after it then, with the hounds. One time the people around here chased a hare, a big doe, down to the river with the hounds and all. One of the dogs wounded her, bit a lump out of her head, but when the people looked for her, she was gone. Vanished into the air.

I had met Rita six months before.

She's huddled into a corner of Lassiter's with her mug of tea and a paperback. When I ask if I can share her table, she scowls at me but I sit anyway. I've seen her before, I like her slender fingers and her pale, sad face. We talk.

'So, what do you do with yourself?' I ask.

'I'm studying English, at the university', she says. This turns out to be a lie.

'I'm a pianist', I say, and she laughs out loud, then shelters her mouth with her hand. 'Well, some time pianist and some time piano-tuner'.

We sit and talk until the café closes and we're forced out onto the footpath.

'You're going to walk me home', she says, looking up at me from under her eyelids, her dark fringe falling like a raven's wing over her forehead.

We're vicious when we wrap ourselves around each other that night; I get my first taste of Rita's appetite. Her kisses are angry – the force of them makes me feel that there's something inside me that she needs to cancel out. She kisses me until my mouth is sore and there's a pink rash around her lips. It makes them look plumper. I pin her arms over her head and bite at the orb of her breast, but she wriggles from my grip and claws at my back, bucking like a small animal. Over time, I grow to know all of her narrow body and the hollows of her cold skin.

There's a story of a one-eyed hare. A hermit living on a mountain heard about him, this fine hare, a big fella, who lived beside the Black Lough. He decided to kill him, to have him for himself. He hid behind a rock at sunset and the hare came bounding down the hill. But when the hermit saw him he was rooted to the spot. The hare's one eye was right in the centre of his forehead and it glowed red. The hare dived into the Black Lough, down to the Other World, which was where he'd come from. The water in the lake turned to the colour of blood and then it went back to blue. The hermit told his story all over but people just said he was mad.

Rita is only ever strong when we're in bed together. In the rest of life she cowers: she barely looks at shop assistants when she buys something, and prefers that I do the ordering in cafés and pubs. She never questions me about my home place and she doesn't discuss her own. Some weekends I go home to visit my father. I make sure to bring back a small present for Rita each time: a scallop shell, a jackdaw's feather, a stone covered with curls of moss. This one time, I bring her a grey hare's foot.

'What's that for?' she asks, kneading its length with her fingers, pressing down on the soft fur then ruffling it up again.

'It's a hare's foot. For you. For luck'.

She pats and pets it and asks where the rest of the hare has got to.

'Luck', she whispers, pulling the small foot across her cheek. 'Unlucky for some'.

One spring evening, I get delayed at work when I have arranged to meet Rita. A German piano has been brought in that only I can fix and I have to stay and deal with it. It's late when I call to Rita's flat and she won't open the door to me. I stand in the hallway, my cheek pressed to the cold, perspiring wood of the door, imagining her cheek on the other side, level with mine.

'Rita'. There's no answer but I know she's in there. I call louder and knock on the door. 'Rita, let me in. I had a lot to do, I'm sorry. Rita'. I hear her laugh, a low savage sound. Then there's the sound of glass breaking. She starts to fling things at the door. I jump back. 'Rita, let me in'. I pound on the door, knowing that her neighbours will hear, but not caring enough to stop.

'Go away', she screeches. 'Go away'.

'Rita, please, just let me in'.

'No, no, no'.

I run from there, hurtling down the stairs, and go back to my own place. I try not to think about Rita over the days that follow. A week later, she arrives at my door near midnight, holding a daffodil wrapped in damp newspaper. I stare at her, silent, not knowing what to say. She brazens back, the two black crescents under her eyes looking darker than ever. She thrusts the flower at my chest. I take it and she flings herself at me, wrapping the wire of her legs around mine.

'Tell me about the hare', she says, into my neck.

My father teaches me how to trap hares. He catches them – alive – using box-traps that he makes himself.

'No point in killing them badly', he says. 'You don't want them squirming in a leg-trap, making a mess of themselves. They're cruel, those things. Anyway, it ruins the flavour of the meat if they die slowly. Or afraid'.

He makes the traps in the garage under the wan glow of a forty watt bulb. He lashes together sheets of wire-mesh to make a sort of cage, one that the hares won't be afraid to slip into. They don't like tight spaces. The garage is my father's cold, sacred place, rotten with the smell of oil and metal and wood chips. His car lives out in the driveway, suffering the rain and frost. He changed from trapping rabbits to hares after my mother died, he needed the distraction and draw of a challenge. But he soon found that the hares wouldn't go into the heavy wooden rabbit traps he used to make, so he began to make the light metal ones.

He goes out just before dusk to set the traps – only one or two – and returns at sunrise to see how he's done. When I'm home, I sometimes ask if I can go with him, but he never usually answers. One night, shortly before the day of the rowing accident, he agrees to let me come.

'Stay with me, son', he says. We shuffle threw the dew and mud, me following him close behind. 'He'll be lying low in the scrape, sleeping with one eye open, waiting for the dark'.

While we bait and set the traps he croons his stories of shape-changing hares and suckling leverets and I listen to it all. My father doesn't say much, but when it comes to rabbits and hares and traps he can't say enough.

The hare likes its own company, they say. It's a type of a loner. That one that got away, the doe by the river, well they never found her, you know. But what they did find was a wounded woman, gashed in the exact same spot on her head as the hare, and she was hiding in an old house, a ruin. Well, she was a madwoman wasn't she? She could change herself to suit herself. She could fool everyone.

We return to the traps at dawn. I'm groggy-eyed and moody, wishing I was still asleep, wrapped in the comfort of my bed. One of the traps is leaping. We sidle up to it and I bend down to look, swinging my torch so that I can see better. My father slaps the beam away, hissing at me not to be so stupid. He goes closer and kneels in front of the trap. He bends low to look inside.

'We've caught a doe', he says, and I crouch beside him to see her. She's beautiful. I can make out her pale underbelly in the faded light and the sheen from her glassy eyes. 'I might make a stew with this one', my father says, and I fall backwards, reminded of our reason for being there. When I right myself and look into the trap again, the hare is still. She seems frozen. My father unhitches the door, reaches in and grabs her by the hind legs. 'The colour of her', he says, holding her high for me to see, 'she's a strange one'.

He bags her up, lowering her into the sack, and strides off through the grass. The other trap we had set is empty. I pick it up and follow him back to the car. My father's breathing comes heavy, with the effort, probably, and the excitement. He talks about the new bait he's planning to use – apples doused in vanilla essence – says he read about it somewhere.

'That sounds exotic', I say, 'like some sort of dessert'.

'Well, it does the trick by all accounts'.

He lowers the sack with the hare into the back seat of the car. I pack the traps into the boot. My father drives and I turn a little in my seat, to watch him: his plain face, his concentration. He looks like so many other fathers, so many other old men. Put a pair of pyjamas on him and he wouldn't seem out of place in an old folks' home. The thought is depressing. He has told me enough times that he doesn't want to end up in a home, a waiting-room. Waiting to die. He says he'd rather a smack of a bus. Crunching the handbrake, he pulls into the driveway, stops and says, 'Now'.

I heave our bundle onto the bench in the garage. There is no movement from it. Under the depressing light my father pulls the doe, feet first, from the sack and snaps her neck with one awful twist. He lays her out on the bench and goes to the kitchen to get the knife he uses for skinning. I pet the length of the hare's warm belly – my fingers getting lost in the down of her fur – and feel right down to her fleshiest part and the nub of tiny teats. I caress the tuft of her cottontail, the black tips of her ears, and wonder if her babies are in the field, huddled in a form, waiting for her. My father comes back whistling.

'We'll eat well tonight, son', he says, and laughs.

'Can I have the hare's foot?' I ask. 'Just one foot?'

'Her foot? For what?'

'I don't know, as a souvenir'. I pause. 'Well, I want to give it to Rita'.

He raises his eyes at me. 'Rita, is it? Rita? Well, you kept that quiet'. He laughs, slicing into the sinew and bone. The crack of the knife makes me feel sick. 'For Rita', he says, and bows to me as he hands over the foot. I take it. The hare's blood is as dark as wine on my fingers.

You'd hear a lot about the white hare. You can imagine it – as pale as bone – it would stand out. People used to say that if a white hare was seen in the morning time, anywhere near a house, that someone in that family was going to die that day. That's what they said. It would be like a silent banshee, the white hare, warning them to expect a death.

I pull Rita out of the boat. She smells of sick and she's floppy in my arms.

'Get up, Rita, get up, will you?'

But she won't respond, so I half-sit, half-lie her on the grass. Crowds are lining the riverbank and two men lift the injured swimmer onto the grass beside us. The girl's cheeks are purple-grey and I know that she's dead. I urge Rita to wake up and I take her hands in mine to rub some heat into them. Her fist is closed around something and, when I manage to prise it open, I find the grey hare's foot.

The hospital's dun blocks are stacked one behind the other under a ballet of swinging cranes. I go there to see Rita every other week. She slinks further back into her chair each time I visit. There's no partition between us, just a long bench with the patients on one side and us on the other. Rita wasn't found guilty of anything, nothing like that, but the whole thing dragged her under. The swimmer who was killed was a student. She had studied English at the university and they said that she was gifted.

One afternoon, when I visit, Rita tells me that she's found God.

'Where was he hiding?' I ask, a joke she'd have liked before.

'Actually, it's God's Mother who loves me the best', she says, sifting her fingers through her hair and giving me a sly look.

Then she lunges at me. She comes right across the long table and punches me in the chest. I topple back in my chair and thump to the floor. She laughs. It sounds like keening, pitched and hysterical.

'That's-for-the-luck!' she shouts down at me, lashing her hand through the air to emphasise each word.

I scrabble around trying to get up. Pulling myself to my feet, my hand reaches to feel the bump on my backside where I hit the floor. Two nurses rush to calm Rita. They take her arms, flanking each side of her; one of them smiles and nods at me. I move away and they guide Rita down the room, back to her own small space. She doesn't look back and I realise that I have grown tired of the anger that hangs like a veil between Rita and me.

I leave the hospital and take the next bus home to be with my father.

JACQUES D'ARC'S DREAM

Isabelle said I should ignore it, but how could I? It was the darkest dream that I'd ever had and I've had many. My wife doesn't dream, or so she claims. Some of mine come to me over and over. Like the one where I step off the riverbank onto a boat, but instead of reaching the boat I fall down, down, down towards the water. I never plunge into its weight, never gulp for breath through filling lungs. I always wake up gasping.

But this dream was different. It was life-like and frightening in a way that I hadn't experienced before, it stretched out before me like the scenes in a play. I told Isabelle every detail of it as soon as I awoke. She lay beside me and listened, never saying a word, her nightcap as snug on her hair as a nest around eggs. Later, I retold it to Jacquemin, Jean and Pierre, my sons. I was worried. This is what I said:

The dream was about Joan. In it she was older than she is now, not by much, a year or two maybe, she looked about eighteen years old. She wore her red dress, the one your mother made for her after returning from pilgrimage. In this dream I saw Joan leave Domrémy, I somehow knew that she was leaving here forever. She was alone, she would never return, and we couldn't stop her. All of this I could tell.

I saw her then in the company of an army, there were many hundred horsemen. Her hair was shorn like a boy's and she wore pants and a tunic, tightly laced to preserve her. What is worse, while leading this army into battle, she was shot down by an archer. But I saw her rise from the ground almost as soon as she was hit – she had only a leg wound. She pulled the arrow from her flesh and before my very eyes the torn skin closed together, sucking her blood back inside, healing itself.

Parts of the dream are blurry.

I saw Joan bow before a king. She spoke to him and his face glowed as he listened to her words. This time she wore armour and held a sword, the hilt of it almost as big as herself. I saw her then on a white horse, holding a banner blazing with angels, she expelled some wantons from an army camp. They cursed at her, their long hair flying in the wind as they ran, but Joan just shouted after them: Your Lord forgives you!

I paused and hung my head. The worst part of my dream was still to be told. My sons stared at me and moved in their seats.

'Is there more, father?' Pierre asked. I nodded. 'Go on', he urged.

The last part of my vision – my dream – is the most awful, my sons. It took place in Rouen, I recognised it though I have never been there. I saw your sister being dragged in chains through the market square, a mob called to her, jeering at her, a mere child. She did not answer or raise her head to them. Foreign soldiers – Englishmen – tied her to a pillar that was cluttered all around with firewood. There was a large crowd gathered: men, women, even children. Their faces were ugly, they leered and abused. Joan's crimes – whatever they were – were read to her, I couldn't hear them. She listened calmly. Then she spoke herself, though I couldn't make out the words. Or maybe I simply can't remember them. As

*she spoke she wept, then a crucifix was laid before her and then …
and then … a man stepped forward and lit the wood at her feet.*

My daughter's feet.

*The flames rushed and she was quickly hidden among them. I
could no longer see her, my only girl, not her legs, not her body,
not her face. Above the crack and whirr of the fire that swallowed
her, I heard Joan call 'Jesus! Jesus!' over and over again. It was a
prayer.*

Then I woke up.

My sons didn't speak, they looked from each other to me.

'If Joan ever tries to leave us', I said, 'if she ever tries to
leave Domrémy, you must take her down to the river and
drown her. You must hold her head under the water until no
breath remains inside her body. And', I said to them, 'if you
refuse to do it, I will do it myself'.

May God forgive me.

ICE

No longer the dead ice. The lake lifts itself to the air, pushing its own life through. Water spurts through fissures at first, like spits hurled from a half-closed mouth, then it gushes and sucks, drawing the brown ice-sheet down into the deeps. Slowly, slowly the floes sink and the water seeps, then rushes, to replace them. The reeds on the shoreline bend forward in clusters as if watching a re-awakening: Lazarus rising from the dead.

Isaac had been waiting for the water to return, for it to throw itself up above the ice, for the lake to come alive again. He hears the thundering cracks during the night as it breaks up and he smiles. In the morning he takes the blue-painted boat down to the lakeshore, drags it over the wet grass. The boat is snug, well-caulked, its thole-pins and oars are new. He shoves it into the water, skims away from the bank with one foot and settles into rowing.

The winter was a long one and Isaac's muscles bend and tighten with the effort; he lets his breathing sing from his chest and throws his whole body into the push and pull, push and pull. The boat slides like a water-bird, the ploosh and creak of the oars sounding out before it. Clumps of slushy ice still cling to the surface, but they break up and dissolve into the water when the boat prows through them. The mountain hangs over the lake, throwing its black shadow over everything.

It's only a week since Isaac skittered over the ice to Goat Island to visit Gabriel. He had brought the dog with him, but the animal must have known that the thaw was near because he'd minced and yowled the whole way across. He kept slipping forward on his paws, into the slushy mounds that were stacked on the ice. His fur was first soaking and then decorated with tiny icicles that shone like candles. Isaac had carried him in his arms across the icy lake at times. It had seemed to him that Gabriel was far away from himself that day, as if he was thinking hard on other things.

Today Isaac leaves the dog at home; he will fish first and call at the island, to see Gabriel, later. The sun hangs halfway in the sky, throwing down a poor, liquid light, the air is pinch-cold. Isaac drops a line into one of the deep veins that hold the best fish. Some people say the lake is bottomless, others say the bed can be seen clearly on a calm day, shimmering like a summer strand. Isaac's mother used to tell him that the lake was formed when a well ran over and drowned a whole sleeping village. She said that if Isaac looked across the lake on a clear day, he would see the church spire pointing out of the water. Sometimes, as a child, he would tell her that he'd seen it and his mother would smile. The blue boat rocks and Isaac listens to the lap-lap of the waves. He hopes the fish come quickly, he has news to bring to Gabriel: people are talking again.

Gabriel lives in a dauby hut among the trees on the island. He has two goats that he brought there himself. Their scattered bones on the shingle beach are the only memory of the original animals who gave their name to Goat Island. He uses one of their skulls – an enormous buck-toothed one – as a candle-holder in his hut. Isaac understands the reason why Gabriel chooses to live apart, he knows all about the boy who went missing and how Gabriel was blamed, though nothing was ever proved. He doesn't judge, he never really thinks about it, they have been friends since they were boys themselves.

The boat skids onto the grey-stoned beach and Isaac anchors it to a post.

'Gabriel', he calls, but the other man doesn't appear. There's no smoke rising above the trees. He lifts a bag from the bowel of the boat and jogs up towards the hut. He stops outside, listens to the swish of the bare trees and to a bird calling. He shouts again, 'Gabriel'.

No answer. Isaac pushes the door and steps into the gloom. He stands for a few moments, letting the darkness wash over him until it becomes dusk. It's cold and all he can hear is the rhythm of his own breathing. The hut is empty. He drops his bag and leaves through the low doorway, he goes to the cove where Gabriel keeps his boat. Isaac pulls through tangles of thorns and finds the small green boat where it should be, turned belly-up and securely tied. Well, he can't have left the island, he thinks. He calls out again, drawing the other man's name across his tongue, stretching it out; he pitches his voice at different levels, some deep, some high. Still no answer.

Isaac decides to walk the whole island. The tree branches are still empty, it should be easy to see over a wide area. He's sorry now he left the dog behind. He sets off, straight into the middle of the island, bashing his way through overgrown patches with a stick. The air holds the clean, woody smell of clay and it's dim under the leafless trees. He stops, he hears something: a musical sound. Standing still and listening, the noise comes to him again – a clang and tinkle. He follows it, weaving through the trees, and he finds Gabriel's two goats wandering around, free of their tethers, their neck-bells giving off a robust music every time they move. They stop to look at him, continue their laconic chewing, then turn away. The doe's udders are heavy. Isaac follows her through the trees then lunges at her. She's quick and he only manages to grab her hind leg before falling, but it's enough. He drags himself to a kneeling position and ties her to a tree.

'There now', he croons, 'there now'.

The doe startles, but he quiets her and fingers her teats until the milk squirts away onto the springy floor of the wood; steam rises off it as it settles, then disappears, into the ground. The doe chews at his sleeve and he has to keep pushing her head away. When he has finished the milking, he unties the rope and shoves her.

Isaac covers the whole island, tramping over the same ground, checking and re-checking. He stops into the cabin and eats by candlelight, some bread and a piece of meat. When he finishes, he walks down to the shore and stands looking across the lake, back towards the far side; all of the ice has been pulled back into the water. He glances at his own boat, thinks he'd better go back before it gets dark. It's then that he realises that Gabriel must have left the island before the thaw.

My life is not my own. It belongs to the mother of that boy, she wrings me through her mind every day, sure of my guilt. I knew the boy alright, we were friends in our way, but what happened to him was not my fault. One minute he was there, the next he had just disappeared. Everyone blamed me. They'd seen us together often enough, so I just had to get away from their bursting tongues and angry eyes. I moved out to Goat Island, but even there I never felt far enough away. Isaac was my connection with the world and he acted as if he'd never heeded what was said about me, never heard a word. 'Your conscience is clear, Gabriel', he said to me once, 'that's all that matters'. That hit me right inside, I just nodded at him.

The boy was inquisitive, different, an on-his-own-type, like me. He was odd-looking: his ears curled forward and he was taller than anyone I knew. His eyes were the colour of weak tea and he looked out of place no matter where you put him, in town or village, city or wide open space. We never talked that much. At first he would come looking for me, hover near wherever I had found work, whether it was felling trees or jobbing on somebody's house. He was always around, a shadowing presence, I got used to him. Then we started to fish together, happy with the silence of the lake, of each other. We would land our catch and cook it up, sit by the shore and eat. I would make the fire, put together a spit, and roast whatever we'd taken over the flames.

We swam together. Stripped to nothing, we would bounce in and out of the lake, laughing and pushing, flicking water at each other's heads like children. He probably was no more than a child himself. I became fond of him, I liked him in ways. But he pushed for more. One night I let him into my bed and I can't deny that I liked the animal heat of him, his need. He came back regularly after that and I let him come.

This one day we climbed the mountain, looking for a dark pool he knew about, a perfect swimming spot. I went along, happy to please him. The path was shaly, loose underfoot. I slipped a few times as we made the climb, my feet sliding from under me, knocking me to my knees. His legs were long and he gangled on ahead of me, looking back over his shoulder every now and then to make sure I was still following. My breath tore through me and I rested on a rock and looked down at the valley. To pass the time while my breathing steadied, I picked out and named the lake islands for myself: Black Isle, Mattle Island, Hare Rock and the largest one, Goat Island.

'Gabriel'. His voice shot through my thoughts, he had run back down the slope to find me. 'Hurry up, the pool is just up here'. He laughed, beckoned to me and ran on. I glanced down at the lake again and, wiping the slick of sweat from my face with my shirt-end, I followed him. I was surprised at how small the pool was – it was really only a pond, surrounded on three sides by craggy rocks – but it was perfect. He was undressing as I arrived, impatient to cool off. 'Come on', he yelped, 'come on'. I threw myself down on the grass, needing to rest before I'd swim.

'I'll come in in a minute', I said.

He ruffled my hair, than took a few steps back from the edge and ran at the water, he let out a yowl as he looped through the air, his long limbs curved like a leaping fish. I followed the arc of his tawny body, watched him hit the water. It swallowed him up and I stared at the spot where he'd gone in until the last ripple broke darkly against the sides of the pool. I never saw him again.

I had to leave, I'd heard things. Isaac never knew but sometimes I went to the town, for relief. I would go late at night when people were sleeping, sliding across the ice in winter, rowing the rest of the year. One of the girls I went to told me that there had been talk, people were asking about me, trying to find out where I lived, what had become of me. It was five years since that day on the mountain and people were choosing to remember again. I knew that the thaw was coming, so I unleashed the goats and left while I could. I wanted to say goodbye to Isaac but I couldn't, even though he had been more than good to me, more than a friend.

I will miss him.

FOAL

A straw-maned mare lingers on the sward, rolling her eyes at the passing traffic, listening to it swish by. She tosses her head and hoofs down the embankment to the road, she noses the air, searching for her foal's milk-sweet smell. The click of her fore-hooves on the tarmac startles her, making her knees buckle, and she teeters backwards onto the muck. She waits, then lurches forward into the road. Cars careen out of her way, bipping their horns in long wails like sirens calling from the sea. There is a misty rain hanging in the air and the headlights cast a halo around the mare's thick body. Her coat is dark with wet and her mane is streeling like seaweed. She lumbers along the roadside trying to find the wheeled box that holds her foal.

Two men examine the foal, one young, one old. His coat is still greasy from the birth, covered in a slather of wax and blood.

'He's no good, he won't last', says the old man.

'Is it his legs?'

'It's the whole lot of him'. He slaps the foal and he giddies forward, tottering on his unstable hooves. 'Ah, the mother is past it'. He opens the door to the stall and ushers the foal in beside the mare. The air is thick with the stink of straw and manure.

'Will he live the night, do you think?'

'Maybe, maybe', says the old man, scratching at the stubble on his chin with dirty fingernails.

The younger man sighs and they both leave the stable together, their boots sluicing through the runnels of dirty water that cover the floor. The mare crowds near to her foal, offering him her heat.

The mare canters along the hard shoulder, her hooves slithering in the wet, and throws her head this way and that, searching the air.

She stops.

She misses the yellow bog that stretches without end away from her field, the blaze of gorse that marks the boundary on one side, the low stone wall that marks the other. She misses her foal, his suckling and gambling, the way he always stayed near to her. His coat was the same as hers: peat-brown with a light coloured mane.

The men came and took him away and his whinnies cut into her. He was the last she'd give birth to, all the rest were gone. He slipped easily from her the night he was born. She had welcomed the steaming bloodiness of him, was glad to be free of his weight from her belly. He was an uneasy little one and he needed her more than the others ever had.

The men had to rein her in when they took the foal. One of them hauled her up into the middle of the field away from the horsebox. She bellowed, and dragged at the bridle while the other man pushed the foal into the bowel of the box, his legs flailing.

'Stupid bitch', the younger man shouted when she caught him on the shin with her hoof. He yanked hard on the reins. 'You're next for the knacker's yard', he said.

He unhitched the bridle and let her go. She galloped down the field and stood by the stone wall, panting and flicking her head. The horsebox was snapped shut and the two men drove away.

The mare followed.

She catches a scent: a hint of straw and spit, the smell of her own milk on the foal's coat. She stops halfway across the road. A truck barrelling towards her blares its horn, its silver-blue lights hurt her eyes and she bolts forward. Her hooves slip in the wet, oily roadway and she scrabbles trying to right herself. The truck slams into her side, arcing her body high across the road. She thumps onto the tarmac.

The older man pulls the foal from the horsebox. His spindly legs crash under him on the ramp and he falls, but he manages to drag himself up again.

'Jesus, we'll be well rid of you'. The man smacks him hard with the bridle he's carrying. 'Hup. Hup now'.

The foal stumbles forward, toppling down the ramp out into the yard. A soft whinny breaks from his mouth and his eyes rove around. The young man hands him over to the yardsman, accepts his money and the two men drive away. The empty horsebox rattles like a cage behind the car. Out on the main road the traffic is heavy, inching forward, then stopping. They curse and moan at the delay.

'We'll go for a pint'.

'We will', says the old man. Spit gathers on his tongue at the thought of the few pints. 'What the hell is the hold up?' He cranes out of the window of the car to see what's ahead.

'A bloody accident, you can be sure of it', says the other man, tipping the stick for the windscreen wipers. They groan rhythmically across the screen, forcing away the rain. The men sit in the car and wait.

The mare grunts, she tries to lift her head. It flops back to the ground and she heaves it again, wanting to get up. Kneeling beside her, the truck driver rubs his hand along her neck.

'There now, there now', he croons.

Black-dark blood, from a deep gash down her flank, seeps into the roadway. Her head falls back onto the wet ground and she cries from deep in her throat. She smells her foal, though he is long gone.

WELL MET, WELL MET

Three nuns had stopped in front of a small oil, *The Three Graces*. I couldn't see their faces, just the fall of their habits, the saintly backs of their veils. Two of them stood hand-in-hand, the creep of their fingers hidden from their sister. None of them moved and I watched them, watching *The Graces*, whose arms were draped across each other and whose bare skin glowed like a low-hung moon.

The gallery smelt of school – fresh books, clean paper, paint – and the floorboards grunted as we walked from picture to picture. The nuns glided away, two sets of fingers untwining, and they huddled in front of the next painting. We moved into the space that had been theirs. René sighed. I lifted my face to the painting. It was hung high on an unobtrusive picture rail and its frame was golden and smooth. *The Graces* were locked in a circle, their limbs dripping easily against the dim background. I wondered who was who – which of them represented Beauty, which Charm, which Grace. I wondered about the models, the unnamed and unknown who peeled off layers of clothes to pose in cold *ateliers*. Had Irish girls ever come here – as maids maybe – and found themselves among the jumble of bodies at the models' market on place Pigalle, vying for a few hours work?

'Do you want to get something to eat?' René swayed on his heels.

'We've only just got here'.

'I'm hungry'.

'We're eating later, with Maggie'.

I took his lapels in my hands and leaned forward to kiss his mouth. He pulled back and looked at me. Our eyes held but I caved first, as usual. René never blinked, it was as if he had no eyelids, like a fish. I had been feeling something between us for weeks, some sort of absence. He didn't listen to me, and every time I touched him he moved further away. I suppose I knew what it was, but I couldn't name it to myself. Not just yet.

We swung onto the Métro, barely making it through the doors. I sucked up the rubbery, smoky smell of the carriage, still enjoying it after all this time. René sat on one of the fold-down seats and studied his fingernails. I looked away, stacking each of the hurts in my head like bricks. Some musicians got on at the next Métro station: an accordion player with golden teeth and another who stared into the air in front of his face. They played tunes that didn't seem to fit with them, rowdy tourist-pleasing pieces. A third man – he was only a boy really – walked from passenger to passenger, his hand held out for money. Everyone ignored him. We were on our way to Maggie's. Even though she was our closest friend, neither of us wanted to go.

Maggie was American, but she tried to be more French than the French. She sometimes made real onion soup, sloppy with bread and thick with cheese, and she wore a beret snugged over her curls. Her apartment was on the edge of the first *arrondissement* and we jokingly called her 'The Heiress' because we couldn't figure out how she could afford it. For a long time Maggie and René flirted with one another and I pretended not to care. Then it stopped and they didn't seem to like each other at all for a while. I never tackled René about it, though I'm sure something went on between them. We met Maggie at *Le Bouquet*, she was sitting outside under the blush of a heater, her jacket slung around her shoulders. She stood and kissed us both, three times on each cheek.

'You look like shit, Nora'. She blew smoke out the side of her lips.

'Thanks'.

Maggie's dinners were tense. There was usually a mismatch of people at them, strays she found all over Paris. She presented each new friend to us like some sort of luxury knick-knack. We were expected to admire and cosset them because she did. She was an anxious hostess, always pressurising everyone into having a good time. Which meant that they didn't. That night her new boyfriend was coming, there was just going to be the four of us. He was an Irishman, as it happened, and he met us back at Maggie's place. She told me to be nice to him. I didn't really know many other Irish people in the city – I didn't want to – so I had little interest in Éamon when she introduced him. But then I found myself enjoying the lifts and falls of his voice, the familiarity of his accent. René was lazy – he preferred the comfort of his own language to mine.

'What part are you from, Nora?' Éamon asked, shifting his bulk in one of Maggie's delicate chairs.

'Wicklow. Not the town, I'm from out the country'.

'"The Garden County"', he said.

'That's right. And you?'

'Dublin. The city, not the county'. He grinned, the smile crept up his face into his eyes. I smiled back at him and stood to follow Maggie, who was in the kitchenette. I helped her to slice aubergines, avocados, artichoke hearts.

'You're doing that all wrong', she said, lighting a cigarette.

'Oh for God's sake', I said, slicing the aubergine more thinly, which seemed to be what she wanted. Maggie had been taught to cut vegetables by a chef, one of her ex-lovers. He was a hurly-burl of a Swiss man, all flying knives and *cordon bleu*. He was years too old for her.

'What's up with you?' She had stopped her flawless chopping to look at me. She blew a flop of fringe out of her eye with cigarette smoke.

'How do you mean?'

'You seem a little crazy', she said, slugging at her wine.

I humphed. 'Do I?'

'Yes, you do. You're bringing me down'.

'Oh piss off', I said, leaning across to mess up her hair.

We joined the others and I crowded near to Éamon, enjoying the stories of his travels around the rest of Europe and the smell of his cigarettes. I smoked one after a while and René tutted and fizzed, the only anti-smoker in Paris. I looked over at him, suddenly irritated by his neatly parted hair. It was like a child's: shiny-blonde and wig-perfect. After we'd all finished eating, I plunged into the best armchair and chatted with Éamon about work and Paris and home. He was natural, easy.

'We should be going, Nora', René said, after I'd spent an hour ignoring him.

'I'm quite happy here, you go if you want to'. I curled my feet further under me.

'Why are you always being like this?'

His face held the startled look that meant he was getting really annoyed. My eyes flicked from Maggie to Éamon, he looked away, she didn't. I agreed to leave, too fed-up to want a fight. I put my shoes back on and punched my arms into the sleeves of my jacket, we said goodbye to them and left. My mobile had rung twice by the time we had gotten off the Métro and were walking back to our own place near the Bastille.

'Aren't you going to answer that?' René said, and I didn't even look at him.

We shared the same footpath, but anyone watching us wouldn't have been sure if we were together or not. We climbed the stairs to our apartment without speaking. The phone pipped, there was a message. I checked it while sitting on the loo. It was from Maggie. I rang her back from the bathroom, with René knocking on the door to get me to hurry up.

'Take no notice of René, babe, you should've stayed if you wanted to'. Her voice was warm-edged from drinking wine.

'Yeah', I said, squashing tiny flies into the mirror with my fingertips, the whole room was full of them. They cascaded down the white tiles above the bath like tiny mountaineers sliding through snow.

'Éamon thinks you're lovely', Maggie said, 'his *exact* words'.

I swallowed this bit of news, a raw space opening in my stomach to catch it. I was glad she couldn't see me, because I was blushing.

'Hang on to him', I said, 'he's a nice fella'.

Maggie's voice rattled around inside the earpiece. 'Oh you know me, I may not even remember his name by next month. Anyway, night, night, Bora-Bora', she said. It was her pet name for me – she only used it when I really needed cheering up.

'*Bon nuit*, Maggie darling'. I said and switched off the phone. When I opened the bathroom door, René barrelled past.

'I was waiting', he said.

I went into our bedroom and closed the window-shutters. The room would be too warm with the shutters over, but they kept the street noises out. I lay on the bed and closed my eyes. All I could see behind my eyelids was the weft and warp of herringbone tweed. Zigs and zags of white and black, bolts of it swathing away into the distance.

Éamon rang me two days later. I was idling at my desk at work, putting off all that I needed to do. I scrabbled in my bag for my mobile.

'How did you get my number?'

'It's on Maggie's kitchen notice-board, I memorised it'. I smiled, chewed my pinkeen fingernail and waited to see what he'd say next. 'So, are you going to meet me or what?'

'Why would I want to meet you?' I said, my voice becoming playful in spite of me.

'Because you want to. And because I want you to'. His voice was creamy. I realised I'd been going over the conversations we'd had, remembering the sound of him.

'What about Maggie?' I asked, adding weakly, 'And René?'

'Come on Nora, you know you want to'. The line thrummed and danced. I pressed the mobile to my ear and listened to its soft echoes bouncing back to me. 'Nora?'

'OK', I said, and we arranged to meet at the Palais de Tokyo to 'catch some modern art' as Éamon said, in a mock-American accent. He had it all thought out.

We drank tea and ate some stale almond tart in the *musée* café, neither of us had much to say. I was embarrassed mostly, wondering why I was there at all. I pointed out a mouse to him that was scuttling behind the glass partition in the café kitchen. He looked from the mouse to his piece of cake and made a face. I laughed. He stretched his legs under the table, kicking me by accident with his big-booted foot.

'Jesus, I'm sorry', he reached across the table and touched the back of my hand with his fingers. 'Did I hurt you?' He bent to look under the table. I was rubbing at my shin.

'It's grand, I hardly felt it'. There would be a bruise. I suddenly panicked at the idea of having to explain it to René. Not that he'd even notice. I pushed back my chair and it rattled against the cement floor. 'Will we walk around the gallery now?' I sounded a bit manic, even to my own ears.

We set off side by side, not facing each other, hardly talking, doing the rounds of Matisse, Picasso, Braque. The gallery was like a place under renovation: there was an unfinished feeling to everything, and its huge white walls and ceilings were plainer than plain, austere. We admired a wall of blue glass trumpets, I said their uselessness was what made them beautiful and Éamon agreed. We stood for ages in front of a video installation that showed a nutty-looking man putting on, and taking off, various hats. We both sniggered.

'Whatever floats your boat', Éamon said, and patted the top of the television, before we moved off.

After a while we flopped onto a low seat in front of Pierre Bonnard's *Nu dans le Bain*. I looked down on the woman in the bath, the pinks and blues and yellows of the dots that made up her skin luminous under my gaze.

'She's lovely', Éamon said, and I glanced sideways at him, knowing he'd used the same words about me. 'Very Seurat-esque', he said, putting on a snobby, art critic-y voice, and I laughed. His eyes latched onto mine and I saw that his were grey, like sea-water. 'I'd love to kiss the face off you', he whispered, leaning in. I toppled back from him, stood up and said I'd better be going. He took my hand, his was huge and warm around mine. 'Meet me soon'.

I nodded.

The tower ploughed through mist-clouds, catching light along the steel girders and tipping it off again into space. I've always loved the limbo of high places: the feeling that you're nowhere at all and nothing in the world matters, because while you are there, you're unreachable. I slipped into the glass-walled café and sat watching the rhythmic arrival and departure of the lift. Each time it stopped, it belched out Japanese and Italian tourists, every one of them necklaced with cameras and bags. I pressed shapes into the polystyrene tea-cup I was drinking from and debated whether to have another *pain-au-chocolat*. The lift stopped again and Éamon stepped out. I thought how much he resembled a lion, with his messy crown of hair and his loping walk. He saw me looking out through the glass of the café and waved. He came to the door and opened it.

'Come out of there', he said, standing in the doorway, 'that's cheating'.

I got up and he took my hand and led me to a deserted spot at the barrier outside. I stood with my back to him, hands on the railing, looking down at the river and the barges foothering along. All I could feel was wind around my ears, all I could hear was the wittering of the tourists as they tried to set up the best shots of the delights laid out below the tower. Éamon enclosed me in his arms from behind.

'It's gorgeous, isn't it?' I nodded to agree that it was, my chest strangled with giddiness. The falling mist shrouded the view, but we could still see a lot of the city through it. We pointed out different spots to each other: the Tour Montparnasse, the dome of the Panthéon, and far off Sacré Coeur, huddled over Montmartre.

'Would you believe I've never been up here before?' I said.

'And you've been *how* many years in Paris?'

'I know, I know', I laughed. 'René hates queues'.

'Where else have you not been to, that you'd like to go?'

'I don't know, really. Well, I always thought I'd like to go to the catacombs, but René ...' I didn't bother to finish.

Éamon turned me around to face him. 'Come here to me', he said, pinning my back to the barrier and leaning down to kiss me. This time I let the weight of his lips come to mine. We kissed for a long time: slow, luxuriant kisses that lifted me out of my own head into somewhere else. I pulled my fingers through his hair and collapsed against his body.

René moved across the bed to my side. I had my back to him. He dropped his arm around my waist.

'Are you awake, Nora?' he whispered. I'd always loved the way he pronounced my name, making a soft *gh* of the *r*.

'I am'.

'I miss you'. He pressed his fingers into my stomach.

'Oh', I said. He kissed my neck. 'Don't René, please'. I shrugged him off.

'What's the matter?' He pushed himself up on one elbow and turned me over to face him. The window-shutters were open. I could see his face in the dim dusk of the room, the perfect symmetry of his features.

'Nothing, nothing. I'm just not in the mood, OK?'

'Maggie is worried about you', he said, lying back and bunching the sheet up to his chest.

'Maggie? When were you talking to Maggie?'

'We had a drink after work today. What's-his-name was there too, that Irish guy'.

'Éamon', I said, and pushed my head back into the pillow.

'Yes, him. Anyway, Maggie's concerned. She thinks you might be a little depressed'.

'Jesus'. I turned to look at him. 'I'll tell you what, tell Maggie from me that if she wants to interfere with my life and make pronouncements like that, she's to talk to me herself, OK?' I rolled away. 'Good night'.

I arrived at the catacombs at the same time as a troop of scouts. Éamon was already there, in the little foyer, waiting for me. The scouts trundled down the steps ahead of us, skitting and chatting in French, and that was the last we saw of them. The stone stairs went down, down, far below the street, further down even than the Métro lines. Éamon went ahead of me, disappearing around the dizzy spiral of the staircase and then waiting for me to catch up. Once at the bottom, we walked through the twisting cold corridors until we reached a sign over a doorway that said 'Stop! This is the Empire of the Dead'. We walked through.

'How's Maggie?' I said, sitting on a stone bench and staring at the rows of brown bones and skulls that were stacked to the roof. Some of them were made into cross patterns, some into grotesque Jolly Rogers. Each section bore the name of the churchyard from which the bones had been removed.

'Nora', he said, drawing my name across his tongue, pleading.

'I just hadn't realised that you were still seeing her, that's all. René told me'.

He sat beside me, my backside was already numb from the frozen stone. I shivered and Éamon put his arm around me.

'Come on, let's walk'. He kissed my hair and I let my head drop to his shoulder. We got up and followed the arrows that would lead us further into the skeleton-lined corridors. We were silent for a while, looking at the neat piles of bones, our feet scuffling against the uneven floor like rats.

'What brought you to Paris?' I asked.

'What brought you?'

'I asked you first!'

'So?' He pushed me gently with his hip.

'I studied French at college, Paris was my dream. When I was a kid I used to pretend the electricity pylon in the field behind our house was the Eiffel Tower'.

'Poor deprived Irish child', Éamon laughed, 'we were all one of them'.

'So, what about you? Why did you end up here?'

'I came over to Europe to look for my brother', he said.

'How do you mean?'

'He went missing'. He frowned. 'Last year in Ireland, he just went missing'. Éamon shoved his hands deep into the pockets of his jeans, rattled the coins he found there. 'We're twins'.

'God', I said, not sure what to say. 'What's his name?'

'Brendan'.

He hadn't spoken to Brendan for months before he'd disappeared; five months, when he counted it up. Some twins are close, he said, they claim to know what the other is feeling or thinking, even when they're hundreds of miles apart. Not them. They'd always had an edgy sort of relationship. He certainly never felt like one half of a whole, nothing like that.

The gloom of the catacombs was cloying, we seemed to have walked miles along the rough pathways, the walls were sluicing damp. I put my arm around him.

'What makes you think he's somewhere in Europe?'

Éamon scratched at his chin. 'Oh, I don't think that anymore. He's dead'. He shrugged.

'They found him?'

'No, but he would've made contact by now'.

I squeezed him around the waist. We'd come to an open chamber that had a cupola set far up in the stone roof.

'Let's get out of here, it's freezing. We'll go to a café and talk', I said.

He nodded and pulled me into his arms. We kissed fiercely, enjoying the heat of each other's tongues. We pulled apart and I looked into the grey water of his eyes.

'I'm sorry, you know, about your brother'. He stroked my cheek with the back of his hand.

'Brendan was childish in ways', he said, 'full of enthusiasm for word-games and crosswords and computers, but not too fussy about cleaning himself. That sort of thing'. He laughed. 'He was a fucken eejit'. We walked hand in hand to the staircase that would lead us back up into the light of the city.

'Why don't we go out somewhere today? We could be like tourists, see a few sights', René said. He had followed me into the bathroom

'You hate sight-seeing'. I was at the mirror, combing my hair, trying not to snag at knots.

'I just thought you might like to go somewhere. To the Musée d'Orsay, even. You like it there'.

'No'.

'Or, we could hire a car and go to Giverny?'

'I've been there', I snapped, and then regretted it, seeing his down-turned reflection in the mirror. I turned to him. 'Some other day, yeah?'

'What are you doing today?' he asked. 'You are always going places these days'.

'I'm going out shopping. And to the library'.

'Can I come?'

'No', I said, a little too quickly. 'I want to be on my own'.

'On your own or with someone else?' he said, banging the door as he left the room.

Éamon and I had arranged to meet at the tiny bar below the Pont Neuf. We were going to take a boat trip on the river. I had a beer while I waited for him and watched two people kissing on the bridge. They were well into their fifties, both silver-haired. I looked at them, smiled and sipped my drink. I hope I still want to kiss like that when I'm old, I thought. The Seine was green that day, churning past, loaded with working barges and tourist-crowded *bateaux mouches*. I loved the soupy murk of the river, the way the water was so purposeful, almost striding along. The beer tasted good; cold and hoppy. It made me think of Dublin and the rich smell of the brewery that hung like a cloud over the city – it was a smell that you could taste. I finished my drink, thought about ordering another, had a bar of chocolate instead. I looked at the clock over the counter and let the chocolate dissolve on my tongue, square by square. The bar-man polished glasses and read his newspaper. Every so often he looked over at me and gave an apologetic smile.

Éamon never showed up.

Maggie called by the following week. I was sprawled on the sofa, watching a ridiculous film on the TV. She said she'd been out of town.

'Did you go alone?' I asked.

'No, if you must know'. She helped herself to some apple juice from the fridge, then plonked onto a chair. 'What the hell is *wrong* with you these days? You're like a big old grumpy baby'.

'Nothing'.

'Nothing, right'. She took a swig of juice. 'The problem with you Irish is you refuse to look on the bright side of life. You're constantly down about something and you treat happiness in other people as a sure sign of mental illness'.

I turned to look straight at her, pulled myself upright. 'What happened between you and René?'

She lit a cigarette and looked back at me. 'You're too good for him, doll, you always were'.

'And are *you* too good for him?'

'Not good enough'. She grimaced and I sighed. 'Guess what? I've got a new beau, he's divine. American, would you believe?'

'What happened to Éamon?' I dug my toes into the soft arm of the sofa.

'Him? Oh, he went back to Ireland last week, didn't even tell me face to face. He left a note under my door. Something to do with his brother, I don't know'. She puffed circles of smoke over her head. 'Wait until you meet this new guy of mine, he's a hottie'.

I shifted the cushions under my back and stretched my body tight, trying to relieve my sickening stomach. I closed my eyes and dragged up René's face. I built up his features one by one: the neat hair, his eyes with their white lashes like a calf's, his lean nose, the raspberry pucker of his mouth. I built them up, stacked in perfection, and then knocked them all down, one after the other.

Toys

I was given the dead girl's toys: a blonde baby-doll with sheeny limbs and pen-mark squiggles on her rubber belly, some story books, a homemade dolly-cradle with crocheted blankets, an apple-red train engine, and a squat stuffed horse that had a corduroy coat. Her father came to our house with the toys one afternoon, a few weeks after the funeral. When my mother saw through the door-glass that it was him, she cursed quietly, took off her apron and ran her hands over her hair. I stood behind her in the hall.

'Matthew'. She held the front-door wide. 'Come in'.

'I won't, Belle. I just wanted to give you these', he held up a cardboard box with toys in it. 'For your daughter. We wanted them out of the house'.

His jacket had a slide of gravy down the front and his face was dirty with a young beard. He handed the box to my mother and looked straight at her, she took it, left it down and stepped out into the porch. I inched towards the box and my mother flicked her fingers at me to keep me away. They stood close, facing each other, their eyes down.

'I'm so sorry, Matthew ...' My mother moved her hand forward, then withdrew it.

He nodded, whispered, 'I know, Belle', and backed away from her, down our driveway.

I had never heard anyone call my mother Belle before – everyone we knew called her Isabelle or Izzy. I hadn't known that she knew the dead girl's family, either. She had never said.

My mother read to me that night, as usual. She tuckled under my blankets with me, all her clothes still on and her feet snug in fleshy tights. The box of toys lurked by the wardrobe in the corner of my room. I had already poked through them and thought my own toys were much better. I could hear the television's thrum from the sitting-room below. My father sat there by himself, half-reading the paper, half-watching a programme. When she'd finished reading stories, my mother tamped down my hair with her fingers and asked me if I knew that she loved me very much.

'Yes, I *do* know that you love me very much', I said, twisting my fingers into hers and cuddling into her side. 'And I love *you* very much, Belle'.

'Don't say that'. She dropped my hand and swung out of the bed, her face creased up. 'Don't call me that again'. She waggled her finger at me.

'OK, Mam'. I was sorry I had annoyed her. 'Kiss?'

My mother sighed, 'Kiss'. She put her hands over my cheeks and kissed my forehead. 'Good night, love'.

The dead girl had gone missing on the way home from school on a bright Monday afternoon. Her body was found the following Friday, in the woods at the end of the town. Our parents closed in on us during that time, they watched every move we made. In the five days she was missing, her name – Martha Sweeney – was in every newspaper and on the television each night. It was all we talked about at school. The teachers made a shrine to Martha on a low table in the school hallway. The photo from the paper was put in a frame, it was flanked by two candles and a tea-glass filled with carnation buds. Martha was ten – two years older than me – and I wasn't really sure if I'd ever noticed her around the school. But after a while, from the photo that was everywhere, her face was as familiar to me as my own: I knew the crease of her smile, her large eyebrows, the floppy fringe. Somebody said I looked a bit like her.

The day Martha was found, the teachers assembled the whole school in the hallway at morning break.

'I have very sad news for you, girls', the principal said, bowing her head. 'Little Martha Sweeney's body was found this morning'.

I remember it took me a minute to realise that what the principal meant was that Martha was dead. I stared up at her, then around at everyone else. Some girls began to cry. We all stood in front of the table-shrine, held hands, and said prayers.

'Oh, Angel of God, my guardian dear', we chanted, 'to whom God's love commits me here, ever this day be at my side, to light, to guard, to rule and guide. Amen'.

After praying, we stood around in groups, whispering, not knowing what to do next.

'I bet she was half-naked when they found her', one of the older girls said to a gaggle of us littler ones.

'She was probably strangled with a man's tie', her friend said, staring around at us.

'Or a belt'. We gasped and held our throats.

'She knew him, I'd say, whoever he was. That's the usual thing'.

Then the two big girls shored-up their lips, rolled eyes at each other, and walked away. I stood with my friends and we said nothing.

I looked over at the huddle of teachers. They seemed different with tears on their faces, I thought – more like real people. We were let off early and, like every other day that week, and for a time afterwards, our mothers were waiting to meet us at the school-gates, to take us straight home.

It was probably a month or so after he'd come to the door with the box of toys, that I saw Mr Sweeney again. My mother had stopped collecting me after school every day and I was free to dawdle home, the way I used to. I had stopped in front of the sweetshop and was breathing in the mushroomy smell from the doorway, trying to decide what goodies to buy. He walked up and stood beside me.

'Hello', he said.

I looked up at him, his dark hair was grease-heavy and his clothes were mussed up.

'Hello'.

'How is your Mammy?'

I jiggled my feet and hefted my schoolbag forward on my shoulders. 'She's grand'.

'Good, good'. He scratched his face. 'And how are you?' He bent nearer to me, his breath was sour, like old tea.

'I'm fine'. I turned away. 'I have to go now'.

I ducked into the shop. Mr Sweeney stayed outside for a minute, looking through the window at me, then he walked off. I didn't tell my mother that I had met him.

He started to follow me after that. I'd see him most days, lurching his car along beside the pathway as I walked home. Sometimes he'd walk behind me, all the way from the school to my house. I would stop suddenly, so that he'd have to stop too, and it became a little game we played: me letting him know that I knew he was there. I didn't think to be afraid of him – my mother had invited him into our house that time when he'd come with the box of toys. He was someone we knew.

At home, I started to play with Martha's toys. I put the baby-doll into a white sleep-suit belonging to one of my own dolls and laid her down in the cradle, under her coloured blankets. I sang to her: '*Hush little Minnie and don't say a word, Papa's gonna buy you a mocking-bird*', and patted her plastic cheek. I read to her from Martha's story-books, I sat her up on the corduroy horse and pretended she was a cow-girl, yeee-haaah. Then I whizzed her up and down the hall in the red train engine.

'You're getting a bit big for dollies aren't you, pet?' my mother said, frowning at me from the kitchen doorway.

'No'. I careened the baby-doll back up the hallway in her train and glared at my mother.

'Well, maybe we should clear out some of those old things … those old toys'.

I grabbed the doll and the engine and marched away from her, up the stairs to my room.

'Hello again'.

Mr Sweeney had parked his car at the end of our road and he wound down the window to talk to me.

'Hello'. I smiled, swinging my skipping-rope in one hand.

'That's a lovely dress you're wearing'.

'Thank you, it's new'.

I ran my fingers over the skirt of the blue dress – my mother had made it for me. It was Sunday and we were going to visit my cousins on the other side of town. Mr Sweeney clicked open his car door and stood out on to the path. His eyes were wide open and stary, and he kept swallowing as if he was about to say something. He put his hand out to me but I didn't want to touch it.

'Martha', he said. I inched backwards towards our driveway. 'Martha'.

He started to shake all up and down his body, then he lunged forward and fell against me, knocking me off my feet. My side and arm hit off the cement path and Mr Sweeney lay across me, hugging me, rocking me in his arms and saying, 'Martha, Martha, Martha', into my hair. I wriggled and pushed, trying to get him off me.

'Stop, stop'. I could hardly hear my own screams.

'Matthew, Matthew', my mother's voice flew around my ears and I felt myself being pulled up off the ground, the backs of my legs scraping on pebbles. My father lifted me into my mother's arms. He stood over Mr Sweeney, who was kneeling by now on the path, sobbing.

'Stay away from my family, do you hear me, Sweeney? Do you hear me?' My father pushed him and Mr Sweeney sagged forward. Then he dragged himself up. He stood in front of us and tried to speak but nothing came out. He turned away, walked to his car and slumped into the driver's seat, his face torn. He drove off without looking at us. My mother held me close and kissed my cheeks, she kept asking me if I was OK and I said that I was. I watched the car drive away. 'Bloody fool', my father said, and guided my mother and me indoors.

I was put to bed, though it was early afternoon, and I lay there, listening to my parents argue downstairs, until I fell away into sleep. Nobody was ever caught for killing Martha and I didn't see Mr Sweeney again after that.

STITCHING TIME

Colette lived on her own, halfway between two market towns, in one of a chain of roadside cottages that were alike only in shape and size. Each one rested on a half acre of land and her house stood out, but only because it was shabbier than the rest. She admired her neighbours' gardens, as much as the swag of their curtains and the glossy window-frames that flanked their front doors. The cottage to the right of hers was guarded by a pair of grinning lions, their gap-toothed smirks making a mockery of their position as sentries. The front garden of the house on the left was alive with slobbering gnomes, frozen in their work: one fished where there was no water, another swung a net at invisible butterflies.

In her mind's eye Colette surveyed her own pebble-dashed walls and the vee of rust that had slipped like a beard below the gutter. She thought about the garden with its lumpy lawn and lichen-caked path and shrugged at the picture. She always said that if you painted the house once you'd be at it every year after that and, with no one to help her, it would be just too much, too much. Then she would fold her mouth into a crease and choose to be silent. The road to Dublin stretched away as smooth as toffee in front of the row of small houses and nothing much changed from week to week.

Colette worked on the production line in the local shoe factory and the smell of leather always hung around her in a rich cloud. She was small, dark and teetotal, and just as handsome a woman as anyone could hope to be. She sat in her chair by the fire after work, knitting or reading, while the radio throbbed comfortably from the shelf, and low hills rose and fell behind the house. Colette was good with her hands. Her free time was passed keeping her house tidy – an easy task because she owned very little. She would dust and Hoover and wash the grime from the Spode ewer and basin that had belonged to her mother. Sometimes she went into one of the two market towns, to touch all the lovely things that were for sale in the shops. She rarely bought anything other than wool or needles.

Knitting was Colette's therapy. It had taken her many years to learn its secrets, but now the wool fell from her needles in faultless rows. She would look through the thick scrapbook of patterns she had collected and roll their names around on her tongue: Sirdar, Emu, Patons. Some of them had been pulled from *Woman's Weekly* and the Sellotape that held them to the scrapbook's pages was yellowed and brittle. Her favourite pattern of all was one that showed a picture of a relaxed smiling couple: they wore matching Aran jumpers that were knobbled and cabled from top to bottom. The woman in the picture held a fat, merry baby who also wore a jumper. The baby was so familiar to Colette that she considered him her own. She would take the scrapbook into her lap at night, finger the baby's puckish cheek and sigh.

Colette didn't have much time for dreaming, but a little mood sometimes overtook her. Tonight she sighed for a second time, then clicked her needles into action to start on a new jumper. Sky-blue would be nice, she thought, a slightly lighter shade than the last one, and she rummaged through her box of wool to find the perfect colour. She put up the stitches for the back of the tiny jumper and began. Each line had to be perfect, there was no room for dropped stitches or mistakes, because each one had to hold the weight of her loss.

There was a rapping on the front door. Colette jumped – her mind had been sailing this way and that – and she had to leave down her knitting, halfway through a line, to answer the knock.

'Who's that at this hour?' she muttered to herself in the hall. She opened the door.

'It's only me', her friend Peggy, who worked with her in the factory, bustled past her.

Colette was surprised – Peggy normally just let herself in. It was typical of her to get her out of the chair when she was busy. Colette followed her through to the sitting-room.

'More baby jumpers?' Peggy said, eyeing the knitting on the chair and settling into the sofa. 'You should sell them, you know, earn a few bob'.

'I don't want for anything', Colette said, taking up where she had left off, pulling and pushing the stitches into place to get the tension just right. This jumper would join the rest, she would wrap it in tissue paper and put it into the suitcase under her bed. Every so often she would lay them all out on her bedspread. A little sea of blue jumpers. She would fold and unfold their miniature arms and press their woolly softness to her face.

'Well, have you thought any more about what you were telling me about?'

Colette didn't answer for a minute. 'I'm sorry I said anything now'.

'The least you can do is send a reply. Even if you don't want to meet him'.

'I didn't say I wasn't going to meet him'.

'Oh, so you *are* going to go?' Peggy pounced.

'Maybe', said Colette, finishing the line she was working on, then packing the needles and wool away into her basket. 'I'll get us some tea'.

Colette's backside was stiff after the bus journey. She stretched herself out and trotted down O'Connell Street to unloosen her bones. Her mouth felt like it was full of ashes. She considered a quick look in the shops and then, though she had plenty of time, she decided not to, in case it made her late.

'Flanagan's Restaurant. It's halfway up O'Connell Street', he had said on the phone.

She agreed to meet him there. Colette thought his voice sounded gentlemanly and took that as a good sign. They hadn't spoken for long, but they'd worked out a signal, each of them would carry a copy of *The Irish Independent*, rolled up into a tight sausage. She dipped into Stanley's Newsagents to buy her copy and caught the eye of a man who was buying the same paper. He was surely too old to be James, too grey and squat-faced. The man smiled at her and she turned away; a terrible heat rose up her neck and settled around her face. Colette didn't think she could go through with it. She hopped into a phone-box and dialled the number of the shoe factory. She asked for Peggy.

'Colette? Is that you?' said Rosie, the receptionist.

She should have put on a voice. 'Yes'.

'I thought so. You're off gallivanting in Dublin, I believe'. Colette gave the expected little laugh. 'Just a sec, I'll have to call Peggy in off the floor'.

'If you could, Rosie'. Colette could feel a slick of sweat spreading under the waistband of her skirt. She should have worn the other one, it was lighter. She waited.

'Colette?' Peggy's voice was tinny, far-away.

'Peg, I can't do it. I can't meet him'.

'Of course you can, love. You have to, you've gone all that way. Now, what's the worst that can happen?'

'He'll hate me. He'll be angry with me for … you know … for giving him away'.

'He'll understand, Colette', she said gently. 'He already understands – he's a grown man'.

Colette said she supposed so, thanked Peggy and hung up. She had to go through with it, she had no choice, she couldn't let James down again. Slipping into Flanagan's Restaurant, she took a table near the door. She was early. The waitress brought her the pot of tea she ordered. Colette folded up the newspaper into a long wad, laid it on the table, poured her tea and settled back to wait.

She sees herself: a young girl being ushered into a dark-walled waiting-room. She looks white-faced, tired, the birth had not been easy. She's wearing her best clothes: a brown skirt-suit with a matching cap. Wrapped in a blue blanket, and tucked in her arms, is James. His puckered-up face is the colour of corned-beef, but his skin is as soft as milk. Colette bends and kisses his teeny nose and he yawns like a puppy.

The door opens and a couple are ushered in. Their faces are a blur, but they seem nervous and happy. The woman wears a primrose-coloured coat; the man, though he's young, has an extravagant moustache. Colette smiles at them, waiting for them to say something. The lady-in-charge takes the baby from her arms and hands him to the woman in the yellow coat. The man and woman huddle over him and the circle closes against Colette. She stands staring at the couple's backs and then the lady takes her by the elbow and leads her from the room.

'There's the door out', she says. 'Goodbye'.

Two minutes after touching her infant son for the last time, Colette is standing empty-armed on King Street, a dirty wind whistling around her head.

'Colette?' A soft voice sliced through her thoughts. 'I'm sorry, excuse me, are you Colette?'

She looked up. He was dark-haired, like her. Low-sized, like her. She smiled and pushed her chair back from the table. James reached his arms out to hug her and Colette moved towards him. She let her tears plop onto his shoulder as he held her close.

'Thank you, James', she whispered into his hair, 'thank you'.

ISA AND CLOVIS

Clovis was already a man when he met Isa, but she was just a girl of fifteen. He worked for Stiff and Trill, the undertakers, and he first saw Isa at her mother's funeral. Clovis was standing in the doorway of the funeral parlour – offering a sombre welcome to the mourners with his grey eyes – when she walked past him. Her waist-length hair was as shiny as magpie feathers and although she wasn't crying, her skin was tired. Clovis thought she looked absent. He didn't notice then the slight turn in her eye that he'd grow to love, the little quirk that made it seem like she was glancing over his shoulder when they stood face to face. And it was afterwards too that he learnt she had lost her mother that day, that she had been one of the chief mourners at the funeral.

Isa had adored her mother. Her father shut himself down after his wife died and Isa fell away from school. She took on the care of the wooden house by the lake and the chicken farm that had been her mother's. Every day she scattered feed for the hens – 'Chook, chook, chook' – to gather them round. In the coop she reached under their warm behinds for the eggs while they flapped and squawked. Once a week she cleaned out their run and the hen house, spading the straw and shit and curly feathers until sweat ran through her clothes. Then she would take the baskets of eggs to the town to sell at the market, she went door-to-door too when she had a lot of eggs. Her father stayed in his chair, whittling tiny animals from off-cuts of wood. He lined them up on the mantelpiece when they were finished: a hare, two plump badgers, a family of hedgehogs and a wary-eyed rabbit.

'You're working so hard, daughter', her father would say, not able to move himself.

'Yes, father', Isa would answer and pat his arm, 'work helps me'.

Two months after her mother's death, Clovis saw Isa in the town, pushing a small handcart that was dizzy with baskets of eggs. Her black hair swung down her back in a thick plait. The cart hit a stone and wobbled, but she was able to save it from falling. A dark blush rose to her cheeks when she imagined what would have happened if she had lost the eggs. She had a vision of the dusty ground sticky with gloppy egg-mess and slivers of broken shell. She sighed, set down the handcart for a rest and squinted through her fingers at the sun. When Clovis saw her stop in the roadway, he walked over.

'Can I help you with that cart, Miss Isabeau?'

Isa took her hand away from her face and looked at him. 'No, thank you'.

She palmed the smooth handles of the cart, lifted it and barrelled forward again. Clovis raised his hat to her and smiled, then continued on to the graveyard where he would welcome the cortège that was leaving the church grounds. Isa stared after him, wondering how he knew her name. She admired the swish of the frock-coat that made him look like a raven. Then she moved on, eager to be rid of the last of her load.

Agnes in the dairy, who always bought a dozen eggs from her, giggled when Isa walked through the door, she'd been standing in the window watching all life pass by. The dairy smelt grass-sweet, like a cow, and it was bright and clean.

'I see you've met Clovis Baird'. Agnes giggled again. 'He's been asking about you'. Another laugh gurgled up through her throat and spilled out of her lips.

'Clovis Baird', said Isa, testing his name on her tongue.

'That's right', said Agnes, fixing the net around her chignon, 'he works out of Mr Trill's place, the undertakers'. Isa nodded, not lifting her eyes, and placed the eggs one by one into the earthenware bowl that Agnes had left on the counter. 'Give me an extra half dozen today, Isabeau, I'm having a tea-party, so I'll need them to bake cakes'.

Isa doled out six more eggs, pocketed the money and said goodbye. She walked home slowly, pulling the cart behind her. Wind scuttled across the lake, raising tiny waves on the surface of the dark water. She thought about what Agnes had said, that Clovis Baird had been asking about her. What did he want to know, she wondered, apart from her name. Isa flapped some flies away from her face, they always buzzed in lazy clouds over the path by the lake. She picked handfuls of purple lady's smock, enjoying the snap of their juicy stems – they would look pretty in a pitcher on the kitchen table. Isa liked the way the man from the undertakers looked: smart and friendly-faced.

'Clovis Baird', she said out loud, just once.

Back at home, she checked on the hens and put her handcart away, before going into the house. Curls of wood shavings lay like question marks around the floor beside her father's chair, but he wasn't there. Isa washed her hands and set out the evening meal: rounds of soft cheese, hardboiled eggs and oaten bread. She waited for her father to come. In the end she ate without him, she was hungry and footsore after pushing the egg-cart. She sat into his chair by the fire, noticed the latest animals he had carved on the mantelpiece – an otter, a swan and two curve-backed salmon – and then tiredness wrapped itself like a shawl around her whole body and she fell asleep.

It was dark when she woke up and her father still wasn't back. She took a lantern, locked the hens up for the night and prowled the garden and house looking for him. Isa followed the mud-path that dropped away from the house to the lake, held her lantern high and called out, 'Father, father!' but nothing came back. In the morning she checked his bedroom, before walking into the town to look for him. She checked the tavern, though he wasn't a drinking man, and all the alleyways that ran like veins off the main street. She stopped into the dairy and asked Agnes to look out for her father, to send him on home if she saw him. Agnes nodded and tried to smile, but all she managed was a half-grimace. When Isa left, she closed up the dairy and went to see the Mayor.

Isa's father's body was found, marooned face down among the rushes on the far shore of the lake. Hordes of cattle had cluttered the water's edge where he had landed, churning it to a muddy mess. The water had tossed and turned him for a full week and Mr Trill advised Isa not to see his body before the coffin was closed.

'You must understand, Miss Isabeau, your father will not appear as he did in life'. He paused. 'He will be much altered'.

Isa nodded and folded her hands in her lap, she pushed her feet into the floor to stop herself sliding off the chair. She had brought the undertakers into the parlour – the room reserved for visitors and the dead – and the velvet-covered seat was slippy under her skirts. The room's musty smell made her stomach feel sick.

'I want to see him, Mr Trill, otherwise how will I know if it's really him? How will I know that he is gone for sure?'

Mr Trill coughed, though he didn't really need to clear his throat. Clovis stepped forward.

'If I may', he said. 'Miss Isa, I will go with you into the room where your father lies, in case you feel faint or need to sit down'.

She nodded and the two men brought her to the funeral parlour. It was a low building and its windows swooned under drapes that were the colour of wine-apple seeds. The surrounding walls were rich with ivy and a pair of yew trees flanked the path to the door. Mr Stiff met them in the hallway. Neither he nor Mr Trill were happy about it, but they let Clovis bring Isa into the room where her father's remains were resting. The air was thick with the heat of burning candles and incense. Isa gasped and moved towards the corpse that was laid out. She stood over the coffin for a moment. Her father's skin was mottled, like a toad's back, his whole body was puffed out. He was unrecognisable.

'It's him', she said, and walked from the room. Clovis followed her out into the dusty street. 'Thank you', she whispered, lowering her head. Then she reached out, touched his hand and turned for home.

The coop and the run were clotted with straw and dirt. The cock and the hens were cantankerous with hunger and thirst, and they pecked at Isa's clothes when she appeared, which wasn't often. There were eggs in the grass and in the bushes in the garden and even on the porch, lolling in clumps like speckled stones. The nests overflowed with them. The whole place stank of rot.

Clovis came to call and got no answer when he rapped.

'Miss Isabeau, are you here? Isabeau?' He tried the front door, then went around the back of the house. 'Isa?'

The windows were fuzzy with dust, he rubbed a peep-hole in one of them to look inside. It was as gloomy as a millpond and he couldn't see a thing. Letting himself into the kitchen, he found Isa huddled on the floor like a pile of rags. Clovis stooped and lifted her face into his hands, she looked up at him, though it seemed to him that she was looking past him.

'Get up now, Isa', he said.

His hands smelt like clay. He hooshed her into a chair and went about setting the house to rights. Tears slipped from Isa's eyes and two slug-tracks of snot ran from her nose, she pushed them away with her sleeve and sat staring into the air. Then she scooped up the wood shavings from her father's carvings off the floor and dropped them like confetti into her lap.

'There's nobody left', she sighed, her voice tiny.

Clovis knelt on the floor in front of her chair and took her two hands in his. 'I'm here', he said.

The house took shape under Clovis's hands. He worked lightly, brooming the floor, dusting the surfaces. Isa sat on, too weary-boned to lift herself. She stared at Clovis, stared at the animals her father had made.

'I have no food'.

'We have eggs', Clovis said, pointing out the window, 'and chickens'.

'Father and I like chicken, but mother never did'. She smiled. 'She had names for all of them'.

Clovis placed his hand on her head. 'Let me make you something to eat'.

He came back the next day and the next. Agnes called to the house by the lake to see Isa. She tutted mightily when she saw how Isa had let herself go.

'Look at you', she said and brought her up to the bedroom, where she brushed Isa's dark hair out and warbled an old song about first love. 'People are talking, Isabeau'. Swish-swish with the brush. 'You're too young to understand'.

Isa stayed the hand that held the hairbrush. 'Too young to understand what?' she said, looking at Agnes in the mirror.

'Talk', said Agnes, pulling her hand free and dragging the brush to the ends of Isa's hair and curling it out.

'I understand *talk*, Agnes. I know what that means'.

'The Mayor says that you and Clovis will have to marry'.

Isa turned around, looked at Agnes and laughed. Agnes laughed too. They both laughed and rocked until they were pink-faced.

'Then I shall marry him'.

'And I will host the wedding breakfast!' cried Agnes, stamping her feet and twirling around the floor, her arms languid with the weight of an invisible dance partner.

Isa gathered wood from the lakeshore and dried it out on top of the stove. She took her father's penknife between her fingers and began to carve, whittling and shaping a piece of wood, remembering how her father had moved his hands. Isa poured her heart's love into the clumsy carving and found herself pleased with the result.

Mr Trill drove Isa to the chapel in his mourning carriage. The early light skimmed off the wheels and they seemed to flutter backwards the nearer the carriage got to the church. The lake sighed and heaved under a light wind and the May flies danced in lazy groups. Mr Stiff walked Isa down the aisle and planted a kiss as warm as a kitten on her cheek, before handing her to Clovis. She wore her mother's wedding gown, its lacy hem skimmed the floor and she clutched a flock of purple flowers tied with a white ribbon. Clovis took her in his arms and held her close and the congregation gasped. The preacher's words were heavy and joyful.

Agnes had laid out jugs of ale, and cakes bursting with lakeside eggs, in the dairy. All the townspeople came and they dripped fat tears onto the tablecloths. Isa and Clovis held hands freely and kissed when they thought it was safe.

The Mayor toasted the bride and groom – 'To new love!' – and he hugged Agnes to his side, while his wife sucked her lips back inside her head.

That night, the hens cooed and clucked, and the sound of Isa and Clovis's love sang through the air around the lake. The cock bugled early the next day. Isa rose when she heard him and made pan-loads of pancakes. She slathered them with butter and brought them to the marriage bed. On the tray, she laid the wood-carving she'd made.

'Husband, I have a present for you'.

Clovis tumbled in the bed. 'And what is it, Mrs Baird?' he said, fighting to wake himself.

She handed him the carving she had made – a fox and his vixen curled one around the other, lavish with brushy tails. Clovis held it before his eyes then pulled Isa to his chest and kissed her neck under the curtain of her hair.

The cattle bellowed through the fields, their noise echoing across the lake like church bells. Isa felt more than peaceful.

I, CAROLINE

My name is Caroline Crachami. That is a lie. My name is really Caroline Fogle. I measure one foot ten and a half inches from the top of my skull to the tips of my tippy-toes. One foot. Ten and a half inches. Some people call me The Sicilian Fairy, but I'm not from Italy, I'm from Mallow, which is in County Cork, which is right down the bottom of Ireland. And I'm not a fairy either.

My skeleton stands in a glass box in a museum in London, just the frame of pale bones that used to hold up my skin – that's all that's left of me now. On the floor below my skeleton is another box with a glass lid. This box holds my ruby ring, the grey shoes with black bows, my death-mask, a pair of socks, and wax casts of my foot and arm. They are there to prove I was alive once.

The Giant Byrne lives in the glass cabinet beside mine, I don't know what size he is but he is very, very tall. We're a right pair – Ireland's biggest and smallest – one huge brown skeleton beside a tiny white one – two natural freaks. Some people say I'm the teeniest person that ever was; a lot of them used to like to pay two and six to come and look at me at twenty-two New Bond Street. It cost an extra shilling to pick me up and handle me.

My Mama and Dada sold me to Dr Gilligan; I cost twenty pounds. Dada handed me to Dr Gilligan on Patrick Street, outside a baker's shop that smelt lovely. We were on a day out in Cork city. That's what Dada said, we were having a day out. Dr Gilligan met us in the street, he had been to our house to see me but I was asleep that time, tired out from coughing again. Outside the bakery, with cake smells clouding over us, Mama stared at Dr Gilligan and she wiped away snot and tears from her face with her sleeve, but she never looked at me. I looked at her.

'Mama', I said. My voice is thin and squeaky and sometimes people can't hear me, so I called her again, louder this time: 'Mama'.

She walked away. Dr Gilligan held me too tight – squeezing me through my clothes – and he made a gurgly laugh. His breath smelt like meat.

'Come now, Caroline my dear', he said, and kissed me with his flabby lips, half on my mouth. That left a wet patch on me and I rubbed it away with my fingers.

He brought me on the big boat to England, it dropped and lifted in the sea, and I felt sick and called for Mama. Dr Gilligan locked the cabin door and lifted me up onto the high bed, I sat there. He licked his lips and said, 'Well, well'. He picked at my clothes with his hands until they were all off me. Then he tipped me with his cold fingers and laughed. His face got red and he coodled like a pigeon and shook himself. I felt cold.

In London I got new clothes and an old man made them for me and they were lady's clothes. The man stood me on a big wooden table and measured me with a tape and he said, 'How lovely you are'. He was a nice old man. And the clothes he gave me were beautiful: a shiny black dress with a ruffly-puffly white collar and a blue velvet dress with slim sleeves. In another shop I got a hat with a feather and golden ear-rings and I felt happy, but very tired.

Dr Gilligan brought me around to see all the people in Liverpool and Oxford and Birmingham. I had my own wooden caravan – painted in gay greens and reds – and the people paid in to meet me. The ladies turned their noses away from me, but the men liked me. So I would laugh for them and smile, then they laughed too and felt nice. They liked the way I walked, a bit wobbly and slow, and sometimes they would bend down and take my hand and kiss it. Then they would give me biscuits and – because I was called The Sicilian Fairy – Dr Gilligan taught me to say thank you in Italian, which was '*grazie*'. I would eat the biscuits and say 'Yum-yum'. Everyone would laugh again and clap their hands for me, all for me. Sometimes my neck felt tight and I would cough and have to have a little rest against the pillows on the caravan's bed, before meeting more people.

Dr Gilligan brought me to see The King – King George the Fourth – in his home, which was called Carlton House. I got a new red dress and the ruby ring that's in the glass case on the floor now. It was a special occasion. When we were brought in, I curtsied to The King, his mouth made an 'o' shape and he pulled his breath in through his teeth like a cold wind.

'Good Day, King Number Four', I said, in a posh voice.

All the people stared at me, the ladies waggled their heads at each other and some of them looked away.

'King Number Four!' The King hootled and let out a big roaring laugh and then everyone else did the same. I curtsied again and Dr Gilligan lifted me up and said, 'Well done, my girl', close into my ear. He sat me up on The King's lap and it was funny, because King George was fat and he had lovely soft curly hair, but no crown.

'Caroline was the name of my second wife', The King said, 'but, Miss Crachami, you are more queenly than she could ever have hoped to be'.

Everyone laughed again and nodded to each other and he tickled my chin. Then I started to cough and cough and my eyes felt hot and choky. They got full of tears and I swiped them away with my handkerchief. The King handed me back to Dr Gilligan who said, 'There, there, Caroline, breathe deeply, my dear', and I tried to get breaths, but I only coughed more.

Little people are better than big people: they take up less room. Small hands and feet are nicer than big ones. They are dainty, Dr Gilligan said. Men like small ladies better than big ones, even when they only have a tiny bosom. Small ladies like big men, except when they hurt them with their fingers and hands. Big ladies don't like little ladies and they don't think men should be so fond of them. They are jealous of their daintiness and their tinkly laughs and how they fit in small spaces. Big ladies have loud laughs – they go ha-ha-ha – that shake all their bodies and make their faces red like turkeys.

The day after visiting The King I felt tired and every day after that again I felt more and more sleepy. I cried for my Mama and Dada in the night time and in the day time. Dr Gilligan told me to stop all my nonsense because I was giving myself puffy eyes and a bedraggled air. My throat felt raggy and blood came onto my hanky every time I coughed. I just wanted to lie down, but Dr Gilligan said, 'No, no, you have important business to attend to, young lady'. He helped me to get dressed.

I wanted to go home to Mallow. I wanted to take the big boat back across the sea to my own place. Even though I was sick, Dr Gilligan didn't give me any medicines – he didn't even have a black bag. When my coughing got too bad, my Mama used to hold my head over a bowl of boiled-up water that had a minty smell. She would cover my head with a cloth and put the bowl under my face and tell me to breathe from the bottom of my belly. She rubbed my back. Dr Gilligan didn't do that. He got angry with me and told me to buck up, he rouged my cheeks and said I was to smile.

On my last day, I sat on the bed in my caravan, waiting to talk to the people who wanted to see me. My breath rootled and rattled in my throat like a clatter of old spoons, I felt hot and weak. I cried a lot.

'Please let me go home', I said, 'please, Doctor, please let me'.

'Oh, not this bloody nonsense again'. He stared down at me and poked at his teeth with one nail. He found something stuck there and lifted it close to his eyes to look at it. Then he popped it back in his mouth. I coughed and coughed, it was hacky and sore and blood spluttered onto my dress. 'For goodness sake, Caroline!'

Dr Gilligan rushed around trying to find something clean for me to wear. He pulled things out of the wardrobe and my trunk, then stuffed them back in. I watched him get angry and throw all my clothes about. I laid my head on the pillows, put my hand to my mouth and died. That made him really annoyed, when he noticed. He shook me a few times and called my name but I was already gone. He put me into his carpet bag and brought me straight to the College of Surgeons and that's where he sold me for a lot more money than he paid to my Dada and Mama.

The surgeons placed me on a marble table and sliced through my skin with a small knife, I was like an apple being cut up for tarts. They looked at all my bits and pieces, lifting them out and writing things about them in a book. Afterwards they put me in a pot and boiled the flesh off my bones until I was the clean skeleton that I am now. They gave me to the museum when I was finished.

Dada came to look for me, but he was too late.

TO THE WORLD OF MEN, WELCOME

His hand comes so close to my face I could lick it, taste the salt of his palm. Instead I watch him, follow the tweak of his lips and the dog-like pout of his nostrils. I think I'd like to kiss him, but that's just the flicker of want for a man I can't have. His son, Ram, is my sort-of boyfriend. The father is white-haired, his thick moustache always flat and healthy looking. He worries a string of blue beads when he speaks, reminding me of my granny. She would spend hours telling her rosary, muttering while she pressed the beads – they looked like a string of raisins – through her fingers.

Ram comes at me in the hotel-bar where I work, all brawn and puffy hair. I don't take him seriously at first, he's been after my American friend before me. But he's different to the après-ski crowd that keeps the bar busy at night: he talks to me, is always friendly. Ram presumes I'm from America, then England. I tell him I'm Irish and he thinks I've said that I'm Dutch.

'Ireland', I repeat, as if that will be enough to explain. 'James Joyce. Guinness'. He looks at me blankly. 'Eurovision. Johnny Logan?'

'Aah, *Irland*. Johnny Logan. IRA: boom-boom'. He points an invisible shotgun at my head.

'Yes', I say, 'Ireland'.

After a few casual meetings – drinks in cafés, a trip to the cinema – he disappears for ten days. There's no explanation, no calling by the hotel-bar to tell me he'll be away for a while, he's just gone. I wait for him every day, trying hard not to wait at all. He returns nonchalant, walks in one evening at his usual time. When I see him I feel my skin prickle and a frown drags down my face. He tells me he's been up in Zürich visiting his brother; says with a smile that his sister-in-law propositioned him one of the nights he stayed – she slipped into bed beside him. He says that she is beautiful, he makes curvy motions in the air, then kisses the tips of his fingers. I laugh. Ram: dirty old Turkish goat. I'm fond of him, a small bit used to him, he's company where I don't have much. I like when he sits at the bar watching me work – a comforting, uncomfortable presence.

It's while Ram is on his ten-day-away that I start to talk to Stefan, a native of the small mountain-shadowed town I'm working in. Well, really, Stefan starts to talk to me. He props himself over the bar, swirling a glass of *milch grenadine*. He always orders this vile pink concoction, it reminds me of the milkshakes I used to make at home as a child, by mixing a pale powder into milk.

'I want to take you out', Stefan says.

'Oh really?' Bar-workers get this all the time.

'No, no. Not like the others, I want to be a nice man to you'. I lift his arms from the counter and wipe the beer-stickiness away with a gritty cloth.

'No thanks, Stefan, I've enough on my plate'.

'"On my plate" – I don't know what this means'. He laughs. 'Please, I will take you up into the mountains on my motorbike'. He smiles, showing a stack of even teeth. I've always liked nice teeth. 'Up to the Hasliberg in the moonlight'. He winks and I smile.

'It sounds lovely, but I'm seeing someone'.

'Someone? Who? This Turkish man? Pfff, he goes with all the women'. He waves his hand across the bar for emphasis; my smile drops.

'That's enough, Stefan'.

Old Köbli slides into the seat beside Stefan and raps with a coin on the counter.

'English *Mädchen*, I need a beer'. I pull a lager for him, re-froth the top the way he likes, smile and set it down.

'There you go'.

'English *Mädchen*, you always look so sad'. I smile again.

'I'm Irish, Köbli, how many times do I have to tell you that?'

I slot his receipt into the clip on the counter. Plenty more will join that one before I tot them up when Köbli is drunk enough to go home. He chuckles and places a lick of beer-froth on his moustache with the first mouthful.

I watch Stefan's lips pull across my nipple, the smooth yellow skin of his face glows against the pale globe of my breast. We're staying in the Weisses Kreuz, a simple hotel off the main-street; it's his treat. This is my first real taste of sex. I'm stirred, but in a raw way, and afterwards I bleed. His concern is for the sheets, the slip of brown blood I've left behind unsettles him. In the morning he strips the bed, bunches up the sheets and looks around for somewhere to leave them.

'Just put them on the bed', I sigh, 'what are you worried about?'

'Why did you bleed?' He's frowning.

'I didn't do it on purpose'.

'I have to go away tomorrow', Stefan says suddenly, 'military service. I will be away for a while. Can I stay in your room with you tonight, before I must go?'

'Sure'.

I push my fingers through his soft-blonde hair and he throws the rumple of sheets into the corner. We leave the hotel, buy some apple-filled cakes and eat them perched on a bench in the bright, cold morning. It's going to snow again. We kiss and say *Ciao* before parting. I head back to my room in the staff-quarters at the hotel, pulling the mountain air through my nose in greedy blasts. I'm glad to be on my own. I slip into the service entrance behind the hotel and call the lift. It's my day off. As the lift slooshes upwards, I plan a shower, a read, some letter writing and a rest. When I open the door to the staff corridor, I find Ram hunkered down outside my room.

'How did you know where my room was?'

He shrugs. 'It's not difficult'. He lights a cigarette, blows the smoke up at me. 'Where have you spent the night?' His eyes are dark.

I push the key into the lock. 'That's none of your business'.

Ram follows me into the room, closes the door. My bedroom is plain: it holds a slim bed, a wardrobe, an armless chair. There are photographs of my family and some Swiss postcards stuck to the wall. Ram squints at the photos.

'Pretty people', he says.

Sitting on the bed, I take off my shoes. Long nights behind the bar have left my feet rough and aching. I peel off my socks and curl my toes into the ridges in the carpet. Ram kneels on the floor beside me – like someone about to pray – and pushes me back onto the pillow. He strips me, staring into my eyes while his large fingers unbutton delicately. Then he climbs over me, the weight of his bones crushing into mine. His grunting unnerves me a bit – it's animal. I stare over his back at the white-stippled wall, wondering if the new snow has started to fall outside yet. When he's finished, we smoke, flicking the ash into a saucer that Ram balances on his chest.

'So', he says.

'So what?'

'Why do you go with this soldier man?' His hand slides across my arm.

'What do you mean "go with"?'

'Aah, you know what I mean'.

'He's not a soldier, anyway', I say, wondering how he knows about Stefan.

'All the Swiss are soldiers, but they don't fight'. I prop up on my elbow to look at him.

'Ram, you're not jealous are you? Remember, you're the one who didn't want to get too serious'. I kiss his brown cheek.

'You are a bad girl', he says and laughs, pinching my arm.

We talk about home: bits about our families, little stories. I tell him about my granny; how I spent most of my childhood with her and that I miss her now that she's gone. He smiles, kisses my nose. Then I tell him about the summer's night I'd seen a couple arguing on Dublin's O'Connell Bridge. The woman had shouted into the man's face, then she ran at the river-wall and jumped into the soupy water. I laugh and he strokes my forehead, running his fingers over each of my eyebrows. He tells me that his sister, who is thirty, wears bows in her hair like a little girl, he says that she keeps chickens and that the 'men-chickens' bite her all the time. He bites at my fingers, making a soft beak of his lips, we giggle and the giggling turns to belly-laughing, then hands all over each other, then deep kissing, then sex. I enjoy it, the plunge and heat of it, the skin and fluidity and fast breath. Afterwards Ram speaks Turkish to me – a curdle of strange words – and I whisper back in Irish, the lyrics to a song about a beautiful girl, *a chailín álainn*. And then we fall asleep, wrapped limb on limb around each other.

I wake up to a soft knocking on the door and Stefan calling my name. I lift my head, confused, and stare around the room in a half-woken panic. It's dusk-dark and Ram is gone. I let Stefan in, wrapped in just a sheet.

'You are waiting for me', he says, tipping my shoulder with his fingers.

'Get off, you're freezing'. I slide back into the warm spot in my bed and light a cigarette. He turns on the lamp and I see that he's in his soldier's uniform. 'Whit-woo', I drawl. He hefts his bag to the floor and pulls a rifle from his back. It surprises me to see it.

'Where will I put this?' Stefan says.

I tell him to leave the gun in the wardrobe. I get dressed quickly and we leave the hotel to scuffle through powdery snow to the nearest bar; a soapy moon hangs low over the mountains. We spend the evening in the bar of the Hotel Hirschen, drinking merlot from green-stemmed glasses, talking and smoking, our heads huddled close. Stefan tells me he likes the outdoors and that he has read whole novels in English with the help of a dictionary. I'm impressed. The wine plants a glow in my belly and when I'm too tired to drink anymore we go back to my room. I have to sneak Stefan up in the lift so that my bosses, the hotel owners, don't see him. We're both drunk and we fall asleep quickly.

The single bed is too small for the two of us and I wake in the middle of the night with cold-pains down my side, and my tongue dry from the wine. I climb across Stefan and go to the wardrobe for my nightdress – the one that my sister calls the asylum dress because of its old-fashioned, shifty shape. It belonged to my granny and I wear it to feel her close. The moon throws a cold light across the room.

Stefan's rifle nests in the wardrobe among my clothes, propped long and cool against the back. I lift it out, squat low and lay it across my knees. It's chocolate brown, as shiny as boot leather. I finger it, slide my hands over it, the shaft, the trigger, the barrel. I look over at Stefan: he's like a pre-pubescent, hairless and fatless and long. The steel of the rifle is cold against my thighs, I watch him sleeping and think that I'd like to put on gloves – white cotton ones – and pass my hands over every part of him. I'd love to smooth those gloved fingers into the cave of his chest, down his stomach into the V of hair couching his penis, and watch him grow under my touch while he sleeps.

There's a knock on the door. I'm so far into thinking, I don't hear it at first. Stefan moves, throwing his head around on the pillow.

'Let me in, baby'. It's Ram. I freeze and hear myself pant. He knocks louder, calls my name. I stand – still holding the rifle – feeling like a calf, wobbly on new-born legs. The fug of my hangover lifts. I shove the gun under my bed and throw my granny's nightdress on. Ram calls out again and I can tell from his voice that he's drunk. 'Come out, I want to talk to you'.

I crouch by the wall, willing him to go away. He bangs on the door, waking Stefan.

'*Was ist los?* What's the matter?' he says, struggling to sit. 'Why are you over there?' I wave at him to shut him up. 'What?' he says, even louder. Ram whacks at the door and shouts for me to come out.

'I suppose *he* is in there with you', he roars.

'Who is that?' Stefan is struggling out of the sheets.

'Don't open it', I gabble, clutching at his hand. He stoops for his trousers and finds the top of the rifle sticking out from under the bed. He grabs it up and stares at me.

'You shouldn't touch this'.

Ram hits the door again, this time keeping up a rhythm: thump-thump-*thump-thump*-thump-thump. Stefan pulls on his clothes and opens the door, the gun still swinging from his hand. Ram snorts at him.

'What? Are you going to shoot me, soldier boy?'

Ram sways and swipes at the gun. Stefan lifts it towards him, threatening, but I can tell that Ram frightens him. I slip between the two of them.

'Stefan, get back inside and put that bloody gun away'. He shakes his head, but puts the rifle down. 'Please, I'm better talking to him on my own'. Stefan goes back into my room, but leaves the door ajar. Ram sniggers. 'Go home, Ram, you're pissed'. He flops forward onto my shoulder and I have to prop him up.

'I *am* drunk'. He leans into me, the jut of his hip catching me between the legs. 'Don't let him touch you', he mock-whispers into my hair and I struggle to stay standing under his weight. Then he lurches off me and weaves his way down the corridor, slamming into the door at the end to open it. I go back into my room.

'He is crazy', Stefan says.

'No he's not', I snap, climbing in under the sheets and turning to the wall.

Ram is sitting at the bar, his sleeves rolled up; old Köbli is beside him, puffing on his stinking pipe. I'm serving espressos to a group of Americans who are just back from a moonlight sleigh-ride. They are giddy and they banter with me, saying next time I'll have to go with them. I smile politely and say that I'd like that.

'Beer', Ram shouts. I glance over at him, then go to him to quieten him down. He throws a fifty franc note at me.

'What are you at?' I give him back the note. 'Pay when you're leaving'.

'Beer', he says again and throws the money at my chest. He holds up his wrists to show a criss-cross of cuts. 'You've killed me'. I pour a beer and put his change on the counter. He knocks the money onto the floor at my feet. 'Keep it. This is what you want – a money man'. I stare at him. 'A money soldier', he hisses, leaning across the bar into my face.

'Ram', I whisper, 'stop this'.

He snarls at me and gulps the beer, never taking his eyes from mine. 'Another', he says, slamming the glass on the counter.

'Go home, Ram'.

The Americans are watching us, murmuring. Ram throws a hundred franc note at me. It flows to the floor, drifting as slow as a winter leaf. I step back and look at him, leave the money where it is and walk away. I serve other people at the bar.

'English *Mädchen*, get this man a beer and I will also have another'. I look over at Old Köbli and shake my head. Ram slings his arm across Köbli's shoulder.

'Two beers', he calls, waggling his finger at me. 'She has killed me', he says to the old man, who starts to laugh. The group of Americans are silent now, one of them lifts his espresso cup and goes to a table by the door and the others follow, man by man.

'Ram, please go home'. I can feel a sweat of tears moving up my face.

'No', he roars, 'no, I will not go home'. He splays his wrists on the bar. 'Look what you have done to me'. I go over and face him. The cuts he has made on his arms form a lattice, like something woven.

'That has nothing to do with me'. He lunges across the counter, tries to grab at my shirt. I jump back.

'Why didn't you tell me you'd found someone else? You want money, so you have this soldier. You have killed me. I am dead'. He flicks another hundred franc note at me, this time I throw it back.

'Talk to me when you're sober, Ram, or not at all'. He tries to focus on my face but his head jolts and bobs.

'You must be nicer to your man, English *Mädchen*', old Köbli says, belching his pipe-smoke at me. I grab his beer glass and fling it into the dishwasher, then slap through the swinging doors to the quiet of the hotel kitchen. I sit on the steel work-surface and smoke a cigarette; its end glows in the dark. I finish it, breathe deeply and go back through the doors to the bar.

Ram's head is slumped on the bar. His father has come in and is standing with his hand across the back of his son's head, stroking his hair. He twirls his blue beads, pressing and tossing them and staring at me. His lips twitch under his moustache and he shakes his head at me.

'You have not been good to my son', he says. Then he pulls Ram to his feet and guides him out the door. Neither of them look back.

ASYLUM

I sit in my glass box, high above the green road, and look at the field hemmed with trees. The box juts from the top floor and, in here, I am above the sightline of passers-by. I can see the chestnut-thick field and the white wall of the school. Branches are dropping burnished leaves these days, cloaking the muck below them. My glass box fronts my room and, though I like clutter, there's not much in here: a low table, my divan, a wall-lamp, and one painting of melancholic lovers, picked out in white on a sepia background.

This is not my home-place and I know few people. When I was a girl, my brother nicknamed me 'Pitiful-delicate', a nickname that enraged me, though I knew it was a fit. I wear the name now and live the life it has taught me: the pulled-back, solitary existence that my make-up demands. I am an observer. My hours are passed watching swallows, ravens and gulls; clouds, sky and mizzle; rabbits, foxes and badgers. And a man.

The man works for the school; he pushes a wheelbarrow, filling it with weeds, mulch and grass-clods. He walks in rubber boots and his long hair is lion-mane brown; he has a silver hoop in each ear – they glister when the light hits. Sometimes the man comes to this side of the field to smoke and I see his face: it's well made, but ugly-pretty. My heart sings to him and, though I'm concealed, I wait for the time he will see me. On that day, the man will come to my room and take me in his arms; he'll purr into my hair and stroke

my neck with coarse fingers. When I smell his grassy
smokiness and know his heat, I will feel rounded out and
happy.

September is the best month: it holds hope in its thin, cool
air. I love to hear the children hoot and bawl in the school-
yard while I tame the grounds. This is a fresh time – a time
of renewal – though there is a lot of decay. My wife says
most people think about the spring the way I do about
autumn; that's to be expected, I suppose.

They are demolishing the asylum. The school has bought
the building and it's being razed to make way for a new
gym. People won't be sorry to see it go: it was the poorhouse
before it was the madhouse; the place affected generations in
this county, one way or another. The headmaster said I could
take anything I wanted before the place is knocked.

The hall smells of mildew and rust; there are fungus-
clusters on the stairs and the walls streel moisture. It's dim
along the upper corridor and I press down in my mind the
rumours of hauntings. I hear scuttling; I know it's only mice
or rats, but I shout 'Hup haa' and whack the floor with a
stick. Then I find what I'm looking for: the room with the
glass window-box, the isolation unit. My eyes are often
drawn up to it while I work.

The room is serene and empty but, oddly, it feels full.
Sitting into the glass box, I look out and wonder if buildings
have memories. I hear soft laughter; it makes me jump and
turn into the room. The sound must have carried from the
school-yard. There's a picture on the wall of a man holding a
woman; he is caressing her neck. They both look beautifully
sad. This is what I'll take. After lifting it from its hook, I
leave.

FROM LIFE

The Spailpín was fake-Irish, a place for Americans to drop into by the weary bus-load, and for politicians to re-live their bacon-and-cabbage youths. David liked working there – not for the under-the-counter two-pounds-an-hour, or the satisfying foot-ache after a night on the restaurant floor; or even the free dinners and after-hours drinking led by Séamus, the mercurial proprietor. He liked it for the other staff. They were students, mostly, who slaved with good-humour in The Spailpín to top up their grants with drink money. David worked there – after dropping out of college – because there were few other jobs in Dublin at the time and, compared to office work, the restaurant was fun.

Séamus – the boss – was rude, which made him appear more stupid than he was. On his first night in the Spailpín, David heard him telling a gaggle of waitresses that the flaps in his chef's jacket were for ease of on-the-job masturbation. He regularly made statements like that, as well as generalisations on the poor, the unemployed and anyone who wasn't self-made, like himself.

All of the staff, except for Babette, were Irish. Séamus had taken on Babette, he said, because, being from France, she would add 'culinary cachet' to the Spailpín. It didn't matter to him that she was a chef de partie with scant experience, or that she told him to his face that she was sure he suffered from arrested development – he was crazy about her. It was he who had given Babette her nickname; her real name was

Genevieve. David wondered if Séamus had been to see the film *Babette's Feast* and if he'd been able to decipher the subtitles; or funnier yet, if he'd read Isak Dinesen's story. It was hard to imagine Séamus reading anything but crappy newspapers. Babette went by the name anyway, and she tolerated Séamus in a way that the other girls in the Spailpín couldn't. She let him fondle her hair and chuck her chin when he passed her in the kitchen. At the same time she was cheeky with him, which he loved.

'Fuck off, Séamus, you are a pig', she would say, when he over-pawed her. He would crinkle with laughter – as if she had just told him that she adored him – while mopping at the constant sweat-beads that dripped from his slimy-as-a-mushroom face.

David was waiting for Babette to plate-up an order. He leaned against the stainless-steel counter and, breathing deep on the kitchen's creamy, sharp smells – a mix of seafood, boiling milk and good meat – he watched her work.

'How can you stand to let him touch you?' he said. He had just witnessed Séamus sing a tuneless song to Babette, using a carrot as a microphone, while he clung to her with one fat arm. She'd continued milking spuds and seasoning them – ignoring Séamus – and he had left the kitchen, blowing kisses at her back. 'Well?' David said, 'those chunky mitts all over you? It's disgusting'.

Babette shrugged and David mirrored the movement back at her, adding a 'Pfff', which he imagined was very French. He loved Babette's pragmatic skill with food; he watched her neat hands plunk champ onto plates and spoon coddle into earthen dishes beside it, making the arrangement look beautiful. She clumped parsley over julienne carrots, shouted, 'Order' and beaded her eyes at David.

'Thank you, Chef, you are more than kind', he said, lifting the plates and grinning.

'Anything for you'. David went towards the swing-doors and Babette called to him. 'Hey! My friend Liam's looking for a male model for his life-drawing class. Apparently, Irish men do not like to pose nude. Are you surprised?'

He swung back. 'No. And are you suggesting me?'

'You always say that you are broke, and the money is good – fifteen pounds an hour'.

'That *is* good. Have you modelled for him?'

'For him, for his friends, for classes in the art college', Babette said; David frowned. 'It's only money – they are interested in you as an *objet*, not as a person'.

'I'd be terrified I'd, you know …' He waved one plate of food in front of his crotch.

'What? Go hard?' Babette laughed. 'David, you would be so nervous you would not be able to if you tried'. She pulled another order-slip from its clip and read it. 'Anyway, it's mostly old ladies in his class – you have nothing they have not seen before'.

'You're selling it to me, Babette, you really are'.

'What do you say? It's tough for Liam to find a man to pose. Women are willing to strip off, but not men. I promised him I'd find a man'. Babette winked. 'And you are *all* man, David'.

'Stop trying to soft-soap me'. He set down the dinner-plates and, flexing his fingers, picked them up again. 'But I haven't a bean to my name. So …'

'So, yes?'

'So, I'll think about it', David said, backing through the restaurant's doors with the two dinners held high.

Liam grabbed Babette and lifted her up along his body; he kissed her lips and whispered something into her hair that made them both laugh. David hung back, watching them.

He looked around the studio: there were easels placed in a half-circle and he supposed he would stand in the space in front of them. He took a deep breath. Babette pulled herself out of Liam's arms.

'Liam, David. David, Liam'.

'Hey man', Liam said, smacking his palm to David's.

'Hey', David rolled his eyes while he shook Liam's hand; Babette frowned.

'Relax, this is an easy gig'. Liam grinned.

'Did you bring a robe?' David nodded. 'The students will be here soon, so take off your clothes and put it on', Liam said.

David grinned nervously at Babette; she kissed him on each cheek and left, letting some of the students into the studio as she went through the door.

When he was ready, Liam put David standing with his back to the class, his head turned to one side.

'This is David, our model. Say "Hello, David"'.

'Hello, David', the class chimed.

Liam handed out soft pencils to the students and told everyone that they could take their time. David was glad he couldn't see the class; they were mostly older women, as Babette had predicted, but there was one man and one pretty blonde girl. The inevitable looker, David thought. And, of course, the one and only man had taken the easel beside hers. David could hear the scratch and slide of the students' pencils – they didn't talk – and soon he could feel his muscles unhinging and settling.

He stared at the wall over his left shoulder, becoming mesmerised by the uneven pastry-coloured paint. He thought about Caitlín, his recent ex-, and wished that she could somehow witness his après-Caitlín life. She would be surprised, he thought; impressed with him, even. He talked to her all the time in his head, and most things he did were with reference to her and how she might feel about them. Current songs were listened to with Caitlín in mind; films he saw were filtered through her eyes and opinions; or what he thought they would be. David missed her and he knew he would prefer to be with her, doing the ordinary things they always did, rather than standing bravely nude in front of a raft of strangers. He would swap all the interesting people he had met in the Spailpín, and the long, chatty nights in the city's pubs, for a life that held Caitlín again.

The quiet in the studio was contagious and unsettling, and David started to feel like he wanted to laugh. He cleared his mind, concentrating on the painted wall, and the urge to giggle died away. After a while he couldn't feel any part of his body for sure, though around his crotch felt cold. He wasn't sure if he'd been an hour or ten minutes holding the pose when Liam said they could all take a break. David turned around and reached for his dressing-gown. He saw the good-looking blonde girl staring straight at him and, in turn, the man at the next easel staring at her. Fumbling into the dressing-gown and belting it tight, David turned away from them.

Babette sat at the bar in John Kehoe's, sipping a glass of lager and reading *The Irish Times*.

'*Bon soir*, Babs', David said, taking the stool beside hers. 'God, I need a pint after that'.

'How was it?'

'Boring. And difficult to stand still'.

'Was it cold?' She poked him in the side with her small hand. 'Were you embarrassed?'

'Yes, to both'. He pulled three ten pound notes from his pocket and swizzed them between his fingers. 'And it was lucrative. The booze is on me, *ma petite*'.

'Keep your money, David. My father sent me five thousand francs today. "Love money"'. She snorted and waved to the barman.

'Five thousand? That's a lot, is it?'

'Not to my father'. She bunched up her nose and sighed.

'Are you OK?'

'*Oui. Non. Oui.* Papa wants me to visit him'. She shook her head. 'But, I don't want to talk about me. How are you?'

'Me?' David wriggled his bum on the barstool. 'I dunno. I'm missing Caitlín, I suppose. Every day. It's like all my anchors of the last four years are gone; we did everything together. And, we had the same group of friends and, even though she broke it off with me, she got to keep them'.

'So, start a different life. Find new friends. I'm your friend'.

'Aw, thanks'. The barman put David's pint in front of him and Babette paid for it. He watched the white head pull up to the top like settling waves, then took a sip. 'I'm trying to get on with things but it's hard. All I want is her'.

'Look at your gloomy face – you Irish are so pessimistic. It's crazy. You were too young to be serious with that girl; it's ridiculous to hear teenagers talk of love'.

'Teenagers? I'm not fourteen, Babs, I'm nearly twenty'.

The pub door swung open and David saw the blonde from the life-drawing class dip into the snug; she had a vulnerable look to her that David liked. The man who had sat beside her at the class came to the bar and ordered a bottle of red wine. David smiled at him and then tried to pull the smile back in case the man thought he was gay or something, but he hadn't even seen David.

'Sometimes I think you are a silly boy', Babette said, putting her hand on his arm. 'I will help you to have a new life. For a start, we are going to Paris. You and I'.

'What?' David set down his pint and it slid in the spilt drink on the bar. With a 'Whoa', the man from the art class caught the glass before it could fall.

'Thanks a million', David said; the man smiled and went towards the snug.

'What do you say? About Paris?'

'I can't go. I'm broke, Babette. I owe my parents a fortune'.

'Shut up, David; I have money'.

He slid his finger across the pint's foamy head and licked it. 'But what about the boss-man? Séamus'll never give us both time off'.

She peaked her eyebrows. 'Let me deal with Séamus – it will be fine'. Babette clinked her glass to David's. '*Santé, mon ami!*'

The blonde girl at the life-drawing class looked irritated; she frowned at her easel and recoiled each time the door opened. In his mind David had christened her Persephone: innocent but depressed. Her man-friend came into the studio. David saw her blush and she half-turned away when the man sat beside her and started to talk.

Liam came to where David stood and told him the poses he wanted him to strike, lifting his arms high over his head, then demonstrating a crouch. David imitated the positions until Liam was satisfied, then turned back to watch the girl and the man. They were too far across the studio to hear.

Persephone snapped two bulldog clips onto her sheet of paper to keep it straight on the easel and listened. The man smiled, reached over and squeezed her hand; she looked down at his fingers on hers and dragged her own away. She said something to him, ran her hand across the page clipped to her easel, then turned to face him. The man stared at her and puckered his lips. David could tell they were arguing, trying to keep it under control. Suddenly Persephone pushed her chair back and lugged her easel to the other side of the classroom; she brushed off David as she passed.

'Are you OK?' he asked, reaching his hand to her. She glared at him and he looked at the floor.

Darcel, Babette's father, spoke English with a North American accent; he spent half of his working life in Quebec, he explained. He quizzed David, in a disinterested way, about his father's work as an engineer and about his – David's – plans for the future.

'I want to get into social work of some kind', David said, his back tense from trying to balance on the tiny antique chair that sat incongruously in Darcel's ascetic apartment.

'There's no money in social work, son', Darcel said. 'Is there, Genevieve?'

'Money is not everybody's king, Papa'.

Darcel laughed. 'Are you tired of cooking yet, darling?'

Babette looked at David. 'Today we will go to the Louvre, yes?' She switched her gaze to Darcel. 'David is an art lover; he and I pose nude for some wonderful painters in Dublin'.

David swallowed and pushed his feet into the floor to stop himself slipping off the chair's velvet seat; he glanced at Babette's father.

'This is nice for you', said Darcel, his face set in the half-genial grin he had been wearing since their arival, late the night before. A business man's smile, David thought. 'The Louvre is impressive, *non*? Thirty five thousand works of art under one roof'. Darcel lifted the newspaper and frowned at it. 'OK, you guys, some of us have to work; I must dash to the office'. He stood up from the glass table and kissed Babette on the head. '*Bonne journée, chérie*. See you later, David. Let my daughter show you a good time'.

The Eiffel Tower made David's breath snag in his throat when he saw it from the Métro, which had emerged suddenly into an over-ground station above the river. He craned to see the tower's brown lattice of steel above him, then smiled, feeling happy to be in Paris, seeing what you're supposed to see.

Once off the train, Babette steered him into the Louvre and he was instantly uncomfortable there; the communal veneration was too church-like and he felt muffled by it. David stood in front of the Venus de Milo and tried to find something beautiful in her; all he could think was that her face was like a man's. He struggled not to touch her leg – he wanted to feel its marmoreal chill.

'It makes you see things differently, when you have modelled yourself, doesn't it?' Babette said, looking from Venus to David. He was frowning. 'What's the matter?' she asked.

'Nothing'.

'You look like you are in pain'.

He scratched his head. 'She has a gammy hair-do and no arms. And she's masculine, to say the least'. He heard the creep of hysteria in his voice. 'I'm bored shitless, Babs; I'm sorry'.

Babette held her stomach and sniggered; her laughter emerged in gasping hiccups. David hadn't heard her laugh hard before and he giggled at the sound of her. She keeled forward onto her knees and knelt on the parquet, shaking and cackling, throwing looks at David between rumbles and then giggling harder.

'Aphrodite, my arse', she said, the words strangled in convulsive whoops. 'Come on, we will go'.

David laughed, took her arm and pulled her off the floor. 'You're sounding more Irish by the day, Babette, do you know that?'

They spent the afternoon in the Natural History Museum; David liked the whale skeleton with the baleen still hanging from its upper jaw like grass skirts. Babette loved the Noah's ark-esque elephant that lead a line of hippos, giraffes and zebras across the museum's subdued main hall. It reminded her of being a child, she said. As soon as she had said it, Babette wanted to leave, and she barked the fact at David.

'But there's loads more to see', he said.

'I feel creepy here. It's time to go'.

David wanted to stay; he stood and blinked. 'You have the arrogance of the rich, Babette, do you know that?'

'And you have the battered self-esteem of the Irish', she snapped. 'It's totally annoying'.

'What in God's name has that got to do with anything?'

'You wanted to leave the Louvre, now I want to leave here. What is the problem?'

They travelled in silence on the Métro to the Tuileries. Babette stopped into Monoprix and bought two flagons of cider. She steered David across the rue de Rivoli, pinching his arm until he pulled it away and glared at her; she was smiling up at him.

'Narky bitch', he said and put his arm around her waist, hugging her.

In the Tuileries Gardens they passed handsome mothers pushing model babies in prams along the chalky pathways. At the pond, they sprawled in matching tin chairs and listened to a carrousel tinkling in the background. David's head felt warm from cider; he slugged from the plastic flagon and handed it to Babette.

'Knacker-drinking in Paris. What next?' David said, watching the people pass. Babette didn't answer and he glanced at her. 'Where does your Mum live, Babs?'

'Somewhere. I don't know'. She was holding her head back, eyes closed, face up towards the sun.

'You don't keep in touch?'

'There are sentimental parents, David, who want to own their children's lives and direct everything they do. When I was young, I wanted those kind of parents. Instead I got ones who had no interest – a child was just one more thing to tick off their list'. She flicked a hand over her hair. 'My mother never loved my Papa. And my Papa can't love anyone'. Babette grunted. 'Some people should not have children'.

David shunted his chair closer and put his arm around her. He kissed the top of her head and caught the whiff of camphor that always came off Babette, even through the sour-sweet smells of the Spailpín's kitchen. It was the same mothbally musk that had filled his grandparents' house and he found it comforting.

'My Dad's an asshole too, if it makes you feel any better. He's self involved', David said.

'Is he the one who's from Germany?' Babette drank from the bottle and handed it back.

'No, that's my Mum's family'.

'You're not very German', Babette muttered.

'Well, *ich bin nicht ein Berliner*'. He drank some cider, burped loudly and sniggered. 'The only thing I'm German about is punctuality. Hey, did you know that when JFK said *"Ich bin ein Berliner"* he literally said "I am a pancake"'. David swished the cider bottle and watched the bubbles melding then frothing. 'But it didn't matter, the Berliners knew what he meant. It was solidarity. Kennedy was basically a good man, I think'. He squinted at Babette. 'Babs?' Her mouth was open a little, like a baby's. David called her again and, when she didn't answer, he leaned over and kissed her lips. 'Sleep well, *chérie*', he said.

Babette was sitting on the end of David's bed in a vest and knickers; she had a mug in her hand and was looking out the window at the mirrored facade of the building opposite. She didn't know he was awake and he looked at her for a while: at her elfin face and the upturned push of her small breasts against the cotton vest.

'Morning', he whispered.

Babette turned and smiled a small smile. 'Papa wants me to stay in Paris'.

'And will you?'

'Yes'. She put the mug down. 'Move over'. David shifted across the narrow bed and she slid in beside him; her skin felt taut and cool. Babette put her arms around him and kissed his neck. David kissed her on the mouth – it was bitter from the coffee. She pulled away, her lips wet. 'David, promise me that you will leave the Spailpín. Do something real'.

He nodded. 'I will'.

'And that you will forget about Caitlín'.

'I promise', he said, and pulling Babette under his body, he kissed her tightly.

Lillis smoothed the paper on her easel with her palms and looked around at the other people in the class. They were mostly women, all older than her. There was one man: he was also middle-aged, handsome in a quiet way. He stared over at her and frowned. Lillis turned away and opened her box of charcoals, choosing a piece that was still one long dark-powdered twig. She rolled the charcoal between her fingers, enjoying the way it blackened her skin. When she lifted her eyes again, the man was walking across the class-room towards her. Lillis glanced over her shoulder, blushed, then turned her face up to his.

'Excuse me', said the man, 'but isn't Anthony Yourell your father?'

'Yes, he is. And you are?'

'I'm Sé. Sé Macken. I was a colleague of Anthony's in UCD a long time ago; we shared an office for a couple of years'. He pulled at his lower lip with two fingers. 'You look so like your mother, it's uncanny'.

'People always say that'.

Lillis flicked her eyes from his and stared at the blank page hanging in front of her. She could feel a soft grip in her stomach: the longer he stood there, the tighter it got. Lillis willed him to go back to his own easel.

'I met you a couple of times, when you were younger. Your brother is called Robin, right?'

'Yes, that's right'.

'How are Anthony and Verity?' Sé said.

'They're fine, grand. Anthony lives in Galway now, he's with the university there. And my mother still lives here in Dublin'.

'I see'. He half-turned. 'So, life-drawing, eh?'

Lillis looked at him and nodded.

Sé sighed through his nose. 'I can't seem to remember your name'.

'Lillis'.

'Ah, yes, I knew it was something evocative. Pleased to meet you, Lillis. Again'. He nodded, smiled and went back across the room.

The nude was angular: her collarbone dipped like a bowl below her long neck and she had tiny breasts, barely curving on her chest. Her vee of pubic hair was golden-red and sparse, a much lighter shade than the hair on her head. The teacher moved the model into position without touching her.

Watching their manoeuvres made Lillis think of a puppeteer pulling on invisible strings; she imagined the teacher's hands were warm and that the model's skin was cold, like granite.

'OK class. Lightning sketches, please. Babette here will change position every five minutes, and I want to see a full length sketch for each pose she strikes'.

The teacher clapped his hands. Babette pushed her arms high and threw back her head; her bud-breasts flattened out and her stomach became taut, like goatskin on a *bodhrán*. Lillis eyed her for a moment, then tossed the image she had seen onto the paper in fast strokes, the charcoal scratching and sliding. She wished that Babette was curvier, so that there would be more shading to do. Lillis always liked to smudge and dab at the charcoal, creating hollows and shadows on her subject's skin.

She flicked her eyes around the class-room and saw Sé Macken's creased-up concentration while he drew the model. When the teacher clapped again and Babette changed position – hunching forward, her hair brushing the floor – Lillis folded her first sheet to the back of the easel and began a new sketch.

'Well, what did you make of that?' Sé held the door for Lillis as she lifted her cape around her shoulders.

'It was great. Though I wouldn't have minded if Babette was a bit meatier. Rounder, you know?'

Sé laughed. 'I know what you mean'. He hovered. 'Hey, remember me to your parents, won't you, Lillis?'

She nodded and fiddled with the strap of her satchel. 'Sé, would you like to go for a coffee?' The words were out of her mouth before she could stop them and for a moment, when she saw him stall, she wondered if she had even spoken. He looked at his watch, then said that he would love to.

The café was warm from a day's business, the smells of coffee and pastry crowded the air. They sat at a window-table and Sé ordered a pot of tea and two fruit scones.

'So, are you still lecturing in UCD?' Lillis asked.

'No, no. I've been abroad for a number of years, I'm not long back. I'm between jobs'. He frowned at her. 'I'm kind of between everything, actually'.

'It must be hard to settle back in'.

'It is. I was in France for eight years. It's completely different over there. And Ireland has changed a lot in the meantime, of course'. He sipped his tea. 'But enough about me, what do you do, Lillis?'

'I'm studying art history in Trinity. I'm in my third year'.

'Wow. So, you didn't just inherit your mother's looks then, she inspired a love of art too?'

'I suppose. One good thing I got from her'. Lillis watched his eyes; they were greeny-brown, the colour of tree-bark. 'France must have been great'.

'Well, yes, up to a point. I spent years getting used to everything: the language, the pace of life, the people, and then, by the time I was feeling settled, it all changed'. He looked out the window at a group of people running past, already drunk. The girls had swapped jackets with the boys and they were skipping and chasing each other, beer-bottles aloft.

'What changed?'

Sé looked straight at her. '*I* did, I guess. My marriage broke down'.

'Oh', Lillis said, setting down her tea-cup. 'Sorry'.

'It's OK'. He grinned. 'Listen, Lillis, I'm going to change the subject now – I don't want to depress you with my doom and gloom. So, what's Santy Claus bringing you this year?'

Lillis laughed. 'I'm young, Sé, but I'm not *that* young'.

The model stood with his back to the class, his head turned to one side.

'This is David, our model. Say "Hello, David"'.

'Hello, David', the class chimed.

The teacher handed out soft pencils and told everyone that they could take their time.

'Do you approve of this week's model?' Sé asked, leaning towards Lillis. He had taken the easel beside her one. She looked at the model, at the knuckle-on-knuckle run of his spine, reaching down to the spread of his bum; the wads of flesh on his hips, the dark spatter of hair lining the small of his back.

'He's lovely', Lillis said, 'plenty of curves'.

Sé laughed and Lillis watched the flash of his pencil across the paper as he sketched in the model's outline. She lifted her own pencil, tested its pliability on one corner of the page, and began. The slant of the model's backbone and his fleshy buttocks took all of Lillis's time: she fingered the shadows, stubbing the soft, silver-black pencil-marks into life. She was just beginning to shade in the wing-stumps of his shoulder-blades when the teacher said they could all take a break. The model turned around and reached for a dressing-gown to cover himself with; Lillis looked at the stub of his penis, wilting like a dark lily between his legs. She glanced at Sé and found him looking at her; he smiled.

'Who is your favourite artist?' Sé asked, leaning forward again.

'Well, there isn't just one'. Lillis scratched her nose. 'But, I suppose, if I'm put to the pin of my collar, I'd have to say Picasso. Very predictable'.

'Not really. Why Picasso?'

'For his irreverence. And passion. His versatility. It strikes me that he was living his art, not just creating it. Look at all the stuff he did: the cubism, his harlequins, the beautiful ceramics, all those doves. He was an *actual* genius'.

'As opposed to a purported one'.

'Well, I think the word genius is bandied about a bit too much, don't you?'

Sé nodded. 'It is, really. So, what's your favourite work of Picasso's then?'

'I like lots of his things', Lillis said, 'but I really love his version of Manet's *Le Déjeuner sur l'Herbe*. It's so witty and all those emerald greens, combined with that eggy yellow, just look astounding'. She turned her face to him. 'And I adore *La Pisseuse*. Do you know that painting?' Sé shook his head. 'A woman squats, smiling and peeing, it's just really funny. The whole thing is a riot of blues. Classic Picasso'.

'You're a smart girl, Lillis Yourell'. She blushed and looked over at the model again; he was removing his dressing-gown. 'Will you let me take you for a drink after class tonight?' he said.

'Sure'.

The snug was tiny, there was barely room for the small table and seats. Lillis sat on the banquette and listened to the noises from the bar filtering in over the frosted-glass doors: a thrumming television, men murmuring, a woman's high laugh, the chink-chink of glasses. She smoked a cigarette and waited for Sé to come in from the bar. When he did, he waggled a wine bottle in her direction and sat down beside her.

'I hope you like red'.

Lillis nodded. 'Was your wife French?'

'Why do you want to know about my wife?' Sé said, pouring wine into her glass with a twist of the bottle.

Lillis shrugged, said she was curious. Looking at his lean face, she took in the thin coating of grease on his forehead that she always associated with older men. She noticed the wings of grey hair over his ears and wondered what he would look like naked.

'What age are you, Sé?'

'You're very forthright tonight, Lillis!' He sniggered. 'To answer both of your questions: yes, my wife was French, a good Catholic girl from Lyons, with nice manners and a penchant for rich men. Which I'm not'. He licked a drop of wine that had slid like a pearl of blood down one finger. 'And I'm forty-four years of age, old enough to be your grandfather'.

'Not exactly'.

Sé set down the bottle, handed Lillis a glass and tipped his own off hers. They both drank.

'Mmm, lovely', Lillis said, thrusting her nose into the glass, 'a young, fragrant little wine, with a hint of red jellybean, and a certain vibrant oakiness that manages not to choke the dry-sweetness of the vintage'. She giggled and glugged back another mouthful.

Sé laughed. 'Yes, yes. It's a saucy, piquant red, that evokes the right depth of tone and youthful exuberance for easy drinking with friends'. They clinked glasses again. 'You're better at that then I am'.

'Are we friends?' Lillis said.

Sé looked at her and put his glass on the table; he took her face in his hands and pressed his mouth to hers. She shot her tongue against his lips and kissed him back, worming her hands inside his jacket to the warmth of his waist. They kissed for a long time, Sé pushing his hands through Lillis's hair and pulling her body closer onto his. She liked the taste of him. The snug door swung wide, someone shouted 'Sorry!' and banged it shut again. Lillis and Sé broke apart, looked at each other and laughed.

'Would you like to come home with me?' he said.

Lillis nodded and Sé fished the cork for the wine bottle from his jeans pocket and stoppered the neck. He stood up and stretched out his free hand to her.

'Now?' Lillis laughed.

'Why not? I've fancied you since the minute I set eyes on you. You are fucking gorgeous'. He bent down and kissed her and Lillis felt a surge through her limbs. She hopped up and they left the pub arm-in-arm.

'Sé Macken is in my night-class'.

'Who?' Verity looked up from her work-desk, frowning.

'He used to work with Anthony in UCD. Years ago. Sé Macken?' Lillis went to sit on her mother's *chaise longue*, she had to make space by shoving piles of ribbons and hanks of material out of the way. 'Do you want me to help you to tidy up in here?'

'Macken, Macken. God, I remember him now: he's that idiot who went off to live in France. There was some scandal involving him. Now, what was it exactly? Your father would know'.

'Why do you say he's an idiot?'

'Oh, Anthony would bring him here sometimes for dinner, and he was always sniffing around me like a lovelorn pup. Eugh'.

'Really?' Lillis looked at her mother. 'You're sure you didn't imagine it?'

'Not at all', Verity held a pattern up to the light and screwed up her eyes, 'he would follow me up to the bathroom and proposition me. Every time. Anthony knew all about it – we used to laugh at him. Your father would wink at me as I left the room to go to the loo; he knew Macken would be up out of his seat within a minute. Dear, creepy old Sé'. She sighed. 'This design is not taking shape for me at all. Pour me a vodka, sweetheart'.

Lillis found a bottle on the mantelpiece, poured a measure and plonked the drink onto Verity's desk.

'It's a bit early for this, is it?'

'Oh stop, you're like an old maid. Loosen up'. Verity shook her daughter's hand a few times, then kissed her fingers. 'I've remembered what it was: he embezzled funds from the college. That was it'.

'Much?'

'Thousands'.

'I have a proposal for you'.

Lillis stared at Sé. 'What?'

'Oh, no, no. I mean a proposition. I have a *proposition* for you'.

'Go on'. She snapped two bulldog clips onto her sheet of paper to keep it straight on the easel.

'I have to go to Paris – to tie up some loose ends – and I want to take you with me'. He smiled, reached over and squeezed her hand. 'I want to take you to the Musée Picasso, so you can see your beloved Pablo's work in the flesh. So to speak'. Lillis looked at his fingers surrounding hers, at the dash of reddish freckles on his skin. She dragged her hand away.

'Do you want to take *me*, or do you want to take a version of my mother?' Lillis ran her hand across the blank page clipped to her easel.

'What? What are you on about?'

She turned to face him. 'Verity reckons you were in love with her once'.

Sé stared at her and breathed hard through puckered lips. 'What else did she say?'

'Not much. Well, she did mention an embezzlement scandal but she didn't elaborate. Mainly because she couldn't remember the details'.

'Lillis –'

'Forget it Sé, it's all just a bit too weird for me. I don't need it'.

'But I like you. I want to be with you. It has nothing to do with Verity, nothing at all, honestly'.

'Am I supposed to believe that?' Lillis pushed her chair back and lugged her easel to the other side of the classroom.

The phone was ringing when Lillis swung in through the front door.

'I'll get it', she called out. 'Hello?'

'Hello there, Lil, it's Anthony'.

'Hi, Dad. How are you?'

'I'm grand'. He paused and Lillis waited.

'Do you want to speak to Verity?'

'No, no. Look, darling, I'll get straight to the point. Your mother was on to me earlier, ranting about Sé Macken'.

'Oh, God, what was she saying?'

'She says you've "taken up" with him and she wants me to ring him and tell him to "keep his filthy paws off you". I think she was pissed'.

Lillis groaned and pressed the receiver to her ear until it hurt. 'You *know* she was pissed. Look, Dad, this is daft, ridiculous. Sé didn't deflower me or anything; I'm big enough to look after myself'. The phone thrummed through silence. 'Dad? Anthony?'

'So, you have been with him'.

'I met him at my art class, he said he knew you and we went for drinks a couple of times, that's all'.

'You know that something went on between him and your mother?'

'She told me he was after her yonks ago, but I don't know …' Lillis wound the telephone wire around her fingers and examined her reflection in the hall mirror. I look permanently sad, she thought. Just like Verity.

'No, Lillis, your mother was in love with him. She was going to leave me – leave us – and go off to France with him. Only he left without her'.

'Shit, are you serious? I didn't know that. I thought … look, I'm sorry. Don't worry, Dad, I won't be seeing him again anyway. Are you OK?'

Anthony said that he was fine and that he'd talk to her soon; Lillis said goodbye and hung up. She stood in the dim hall and stared at her mother's studio door, before pushing it open. Verity was propped over her desk, snoring, a glass still in her fist. Lillis shook her awake.

'Get off me'. Verity pushed Lillis away.

'You knew Sé Macken a lot better than you let on'.

Her mother snorted and picked a line of hair out of her mouth. 'Steer clear of him, Lilydoll, he's a liar'.

'How original: the pot calling the kettle black'. Lillis hefted her satchel onto her shoulder and walked over to the door.

'Has he offered to take you to Paris yet?' Lillis swung around and stared at her mother; Verity lifted her glass. '*Plus ça change*. Cheers, sweetheart'.

THE OUSE'S CALL

The River Ouse slips and glides past Monk's House, like an eel; the water is peat-brown, slick, sure-flowing. Our house is built so near the river that I like to think it keeps it on its path. I stand at the window every morning, to watch it go by and see what changes have come over it during the night. Some days it's decorated with patches of creamy scurf and the surface churns like a vat of porter. Other days the river-water is as smooth as old stones. I listen to the water, hear it turning and twisting, like a key in a broken lock. Today, after last night's rain, it gushes and hurtles along, in a hurry to get to the sea. I smell the river; I pull its rain-soaked, weed-cold stink into my nose and breathe deeply. I love that smell.

Sometimes, when Leonard finds me standing here, staring out the window, he calls me his dreamy-dreamer; but he also watches me, as if I were a child. He doesn't like the way I fill my hours. Or the way I don't. The weight of my melancholy is not easily packaged up and boxed off, like something ordinary. Leonard coddles me along and tries to cheer me up with bright words. Sometimes, he brings me cuttings from the meadow: buttercups, primroses, grasses – whatever he can find.

Earlier this morning he asked if my headache was better; I had forgotten I'd said I had one.

'Pardon?' I said. 'Oh no, Leonard, it's … I mean, yes, yes. I'm fine'.

'Good, good'.

'But I didn't sleep much last night; the bedroom air frightened me. The coldness of it'.

'You should have called me, Virginia'.

'I don't like to disturb you, darling'. I took his hand and squeezed it. 'I lay there listening to the rain, and I heard a voice say, "You will never write again". So you see, my strongest pleasure is soon to be gone from me'.

'It was most likely a dream', he said. 'Doctor Octavia says you mustn't listen to dreams or voices, and you really mustn't, you know'. He kissed my forehead and smiled.

'I know, Leonard'. I grasped his arm. 'But day by day I'm losing my power over words; I can't do a thing with them'.

'They will come back, my love; they always do', he said, and I smiled and continued to watch the river.

My writing used to spurt from me like a volcano until I was spent by it, and that made me happy; I want that again.

The rooks are here this morning, circling above the water, their pewter wings cracking through the air. They settle on the top branches of the trees, on the opposite side of the river, and watch me, looking like gossipy old men in their grey waistcoats. They remind me of my father in the months before he died: hooked over and watching, complaining all the time. The rooks speak to me in Greek – the same old nonsense each time about Narcissus and Echo – and I have to shout at them to go away. The last time it happened, I told Vanessa.

'I don't believe that birds can speak foreign languages', she said. 'I really don't believe they can talk at all'.

'You haven't heard them, Vanessa. They are verbose'.

'And have you, heard them, Virginia? I mean really *heard* them?' she said, as if I were completely mad.

'Of course I have. Why else would I mention it?'

She folded her lips and shook her head, and I felt rather annoyed with her. My sister can be impossible to talk to at times – quite the cold sceptic.

The Ouse has a high smell today. When I push up the window, the breeze blows the lace curtain into the room, like a bridal veil. It's a light wind and it carries the river-stink right up to me. The smell is clotted: thick and weedy and clay-drenched; that peculiar after-rain smell that's fresh and rotten at the same time.

Two swans are preening together on the water, their plump, perfect bodies doing a good job of hiding their malicious hearts. People love swans; they admire them for their grace and their faithfulness, their white purity. I hate them – they are always so stone-cold and aloof; I hate the way they hiss and lunge. Oh, they are elegant birds all right, but they are chilly and so very sad. It's better, I always think, to stay away from swans, to keep a respectable distance.

The susurrence of the Ouse keeps me company, day in, day out. I let its water-noises flood up inside me, rush through my head and scatter into my veins. Whether I'm awake or asleep, I hear its roiling currents, shivering eddies, roaring rain-soaked torrents, gentle lap-lap-lapping. The river-sounds drench me, day and night. The water is like a lullaby in my ear. I own this part of the river; its mine, my own small queendom.

I leave the window and go to the telephone, needing the sound of Vanessa's voice. I mean to pretend to her that I am robust and well but, when I hear her voice, it is such a comfort to me that I can't help but say how I am feeling.

'Sleep is hard to come by these nights and that makes my mind poorly in the daytime. It means I can't write'.

'You must take your rest, dearest', she says, 'soon the mild spring weather will take hold and you will bounce with energy all day, and snore all night'.

'But the air-raid sirens sing in my ears, Vanessa. Even when they are not sounding, I hear their roar', I confess to her. 'Why? Why does my mind turn things around so?'

'We all mull things over and have imaginings. Yours are just more vivid than most, poor pet. At least you are out of London. How is Leonard?'

'Leonard is fine. But I am only half here, Ness', I whisper. 'And, unfortunately, I am left with the wrong half'.

'You are exhausted, Virginia. Do as I tell you and go back to bed immediately'.

'I promise that I will', I say, but change my mind when I plop the receiver back into its cradle, as Vanessa is not present to insist upon it.

The Ouse needs me; it calls out to me, pushes its wringing fingers up to my window and claws at the glass. I step nearer and push the window further open, so it's stretched wide, like the waiting jaws of a huge fish. I lean out and listen to the river's voice. Leaving the window open, I go to my bureau. There I write a letter each to Leonard and Vanessa, telling them what I have long known – that I am going mad again and that, this time, I shan't recover. I reassure them that they have given me the greatest possible happiness and that I'm sorry to leave them, but the disease is now bigger than I am. I thank them for their patience and I apologise for ruining their lives, as I know I must. And I *am* truly sorry. Sorry for their sorrow and for my own sad state.

Then I put on my hat and coat and take my cane; I let myself out of our house and walk to the river. I breathe deep on its fusty-fresh smell. A wood-pigeon breaks from a high branch, and I lift my head for a moment to the slap-flutter of wings and a flash of grey. I put my cane down on the grassy bank, take off my hat, and fill my coat pockets with the biggest stones I can find.

I sit down; the riverbank is muddy and cold. I dangle my legs over the edge, above the careening water. Now I can hear the Ouse's voice more clearly: its honey-brown, tinkle-tearing, convincing words. It is urging me to come nearer; it offers me its folds to close around my body. I listen to it, gushing, rushing, calling me in. It is the clearest and most convincing of all the voices. This is my life, I think. This river.

ABOUT THE AUTHOR

Nuala Ní Chonchúir was born in Dublin in 1970 and lives in County
Galway. Her poetry was first anthologised as *Molly's Daughter* in the
first Arlen House ¡*DIVAS! New Irish Women's Writing* collection in 2003.
Her debut poetry collection, *Tattoo ¦ Tatú* (2007) was shortlisted for the
Strong Award. Her short fiction collections are *The Wind Across the
Grass* (2004/2009), *To the World of Men, Welcome* (2005/2011) and *Nude*
(2009). In 2005 she edited the second ¡*DIVAS!* anthology, 'A Sense of
Place'. Her novel *You* was published to critical acclaim in 2010 and her
next poetry collection, *The Juno Charm*, will appear in 2011. Nuala has
won many short fiction prizes, including the inaugural Cúirt New
Writing Prize, RTÉ's Francis MacManus Award, the inaugural
Jonathan Swift Award and the Cecil Day Lewis Award. See:
www.nualanichonchuir.com

SELECT BIBLIOGRAPHY
Molly's Daughter anthologised in ¡*DIVAS! New Irish Women's Writing*
(Arlen House, 2003), poetry.
The Wind Across the Grass (Arlen House, 2004/2009), short fiction.
To the World of Men, Welcome (Arlen House, 2005/2011), short fiction.
Tattoo ¦ Tatú (Arlen House, 2007), poetry.
Portrait of the Artist with a Red Car (Templar, 2009), poetry chapbook.
Nude (Salt Publishing, 2009), short fiction.
You (New Island, 2010), novel.
The Juno Charm (Salmon, 2011), poetry.

AS EDITOR/CO-EDITOR
¡*DIVAS! New Irish Women's Writing: A Sense of Place* (Arlen House, 2005).
New Writing from the West series, featuring authors Geraldine Mills,
Colette Nic Aodha and Órfhlaith Foyle (Arlen House, 2005).
Best of Irish Poetry 2009 (Munster Literature Centre, 2008).
Southword, Nos 14–5 (Munster Literature Centre, 2008–9).
Horizon Review (Salt Publishing, 2009).

AS TRANSLATOR
Cathal Ó Searcaigh, *Dánta Grá ¦ Love Poems,* illustrated by Pauline
Bewick (Arlen House, 2012).